How to Make Pants and Jeans
That Really Fit

OTHER BOOKS BY BARBARA CORRIGAN

I Love to Sew

Of Course You Can Sew

How to Make Something Out of Practically Nothing

HOW TO MAKE PANTS AND JEANS THAT REALLY FIT

Barbara Corrigan

DOUBLEDAY & COMPANY, INC., GARDEN CITY, NEW YORK

Library of Congress Cataloging in Publication Data

Corrigan, Barbara, 1922–
    How to make pants and jeans that really fit.

    SUMMARY: Presents complete instructions for
sewing and altering pants to fit correctly.
    1. Trousers—Juvenile literature. 2. Jeans
(Clothing)—Juvenile literature. [1. Trousers.
2. Jeans (Clothing)] I. Title.
TT542.C67   646.4'3
ISBN: 0-385-12786-3 Trade
        0-385-13574-2 Paperbound
Library of Congress Catalog Card Number 77–74295

Contents

Introduction

Dressing in pants has in recent years become a way of life for most young women and girls. It is a rare occasion when some style of pants will not be suitable.

It seems as if pants will be with us for a long time, for modern young women don't want to give up a comfortable, easy fashion that is so well suited to their informal, relaxed life-style.

Practicality is not everything. We all know that a well-chosen and well-fitted pants outfit can look extremely smart, flattering, and, yes, feminine.

The key word here is "well-fitted." What could look more hideous than pants that either pull into wrinkles around the crotch, droop in the seat, or cling to the legs like sausage casings? Some girls are lucky to have the kind of figure that is easily fitted with ready-to-wear pants, but others with less than ideal figures can get the required perfect fit only by going to a custom tailor, or by learning to make their own.

Of course, perfect fit is not the only reason to do it yourself. Clothes are so expensive to buy (even the old faithful blue jeans are getting into the luxury class) that you can save a lot on your clothes budget by learning to sew your own pants, as well as other garments.

You can also indulge your own individual taste by choosing the exact material for the exact style of pants that you want.

Are you afraid that pants are too difficult to make? Not if you let this book guide you step by step with detailed instructions for choosing material and pattern, making necessary pattern alterations and fitting a trial pair of pants in muslin, cutting out your good fabric, and sewing together and finishing several styles of pants.

You will also learn how to fit or remodel pants that you have already bought, and you will find suggestions for choosing the most becoming styles and ideas for building a complete pants wardrobe with co-ordinating tops and accessories.

CHAPTER ONE

Facts About Fabrics

The first step in making pants is to decide what kind of fabric you want to buy. The stores have an endless variety of materials, of which some are suitable for casual pants and jeans, some are suitable for dressy pants, and some are not suitable for pants at all.

What you want is something quite firm, closely woven, and opaque that will hold its shape.

What you want to avoid is soft, droopy, stretchy fabrics, or anything thin and sheer (except possibly for dressy hostess pajamas).

There are several types of fibers to consider:

Cotton or blends of cotton with polyester. One hundred per cent cotton is not easy to find now, but if you can get it, you will find it is easy to work with and comfortable to wear. Many of the blends are very good, and they need little or no ironing.

The most popular of the cotton materials for pants is *denim*, which comes in a great variety of bright or pastel colors, as well as the traditional blue for jeans. There are denims in heavy or light weights, prewashed or prefaded, brushed-surface, with patchwork effects, or with a pattern of stitched-in tucks. Real denim has a diagonal weave. If you look closely you will see a pattern of slanting lines (Fig. 1).

Another suitable cotton is *sailcloth*, which has a plain weave (Fig. 2), and there are many other plain-weave cottons or cotton blends, in plain colors, printed designs, woven stripes, or checks. Just be sure that the fabric is not too lightweight or soft.

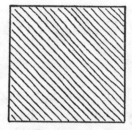

Fig. 1.   Diagonal weave of denim

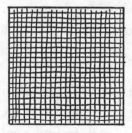

Fig. 2.   Plain-weave cotton

Seersucker, which has a woven-in crinkly stripe, is very suitable.

Corduroy is good for winter-weight pants. It is made of cotton, with a velvety nap, and comes plain or printed, in either narrow- or wide-wale patterns (this refers to the woven-in stripe), and also in the newer no-wale type, which looks somewhat like velvet.

There is a particular problem with corduroy that you must learn about. The nap of the fabric—that is, the fuzzy texture —is slightly flattened in one direction. Fig. 3 shows an enlarged cross section.

Fig. 3.   Cross section of napped fabric

When cutting a garment out of corduroy, you must be sure that all the pattern pieces face in the same direction. Your pattern layout will be labeled "for fabrics *with nap*," and this will also be specified in the yardage requirements on the back of the pattern envelope.

The reason for this is that if the nap is facing up in some sections and down in others, the upward-facing section looks much darker than the other, because of the way it reflects the light (Fig. 4). This makes it obvious that the garment was made by an amateur who didn't know what she was doing.

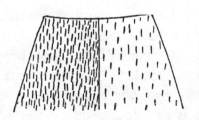

Fig. 4.   Napped fabric facing in opposite directions

Anything cut out of material "with nap" always requires extra yardage, because the pattern pieces cannot be fitted together so economically.

Wool. For winter pants, wool is perfect. Do not choose a soft, loose weave. The kind called *worsted* has a smooth, hard finish and is often used for men's suits. *Flannel, gabardine,* and firm *tweeds* are also suitable. Wool with a bonded backing of another material is fine, especially if wool makes you itch. If you have this trouble, wool pants should be lined. You will learn more about this in a later chapter.

Wool is often blended with varying proportions of polyester or nylon, which makes it quite wrinkle-free and often washable.

Acrylic is a synthetic fiber, similar to wool, but without the itchiness. It is also washable.

Knits. Polyester double-knit is a perfect pants material. It is easy to work with, holds its shape well, and comes in plain colors and many patterns, some of which look very much like woven wool. It is very comfortable to wear because it stretches, yet it snaps back to shape. It washes beautifully.

Wool knits are not quite so good because they tend to become baggy with wear.

A fairly new material is a woven *polyester gabardine.* It is smooth, with a faint diagonal weave, like denim, and is firm but lightweight. It comes in many plain colors, checks, and plaids.

Before cutting out your pants, you must be very sure that the material is not going to shrink. Cottons in particular may be a problem. Of course, when you buy ready-made blue jeans you plan to shrink them so they will be very snug, but if you make your own you can fit them perfectly in the first place. If there is any doubt, shrink the fabric by putting it through the washing machine or by hand washing, whichever method you would normally use on cotton clothes.

Synthetics are usually no problem, but wool may or may not have been preshrunk. If you are not sure, the best thing is to take it to a dry cleaner and ask to have it "sponged and shrunk."

A few words here about other sewing materials and equipment:

Thread. Although manufacturers are trying hard to push polyester thread now, I think most of it is of a very poor quality. It is rough and fuzzy and hard to sew with either in the machine or by hand; plain old *mercerized cotton* works better, even on synthetics. Polyester thread is supposed to have more stretch for knit fabrics, but this is not needed if your sewing machine has a stretch stitch or even a plain zigzag.

Thread made with a polyester core covered with cotton is more satisfactory than 100 per cent polyester.

Zippers. Metal, nylon, or polyester zippers are all okay. There are heavy-duty metal zippers made especially for pants.

You can often find bargains in zippers that have been taken out of their packages. They are just as good and will save you a lot of money.

Interfacing. This is the name for any of several kinds of material used for stiffening waistbands, pockets, and so on. It is important to use this wherever it is called for, to get professional results.

It comes in several types of fiber, and in light, medium, or heavy weights. There are woven cotton or synthetic fabrics, a non-woven fiber with a crisp finish (there are several brand names for this), and the newer fusible types, which can be permanently bonded to your fabric with a steam iron. Most people find these are the easiest to work with, although they do cost more than the regular non-fusible.

Your sewing tools should be the best you can afford and kept in good condition. The sewing machine is most important, and you should learn how to clean and oil it. Machine needles should be changed fairly often, and you should have an assortment of different sizes for light and heavy fabrics.

Good dressmaker's shears are essential, seven or eight inches long, with a bent handle (Fig. 5). Small pointed scissors are also useful.

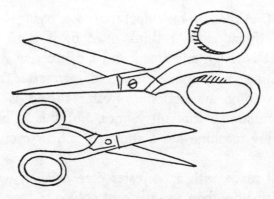

Fig. 5.   Dressmaker's shears and small scissors

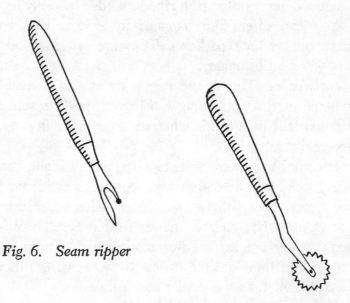

Fig. 6.   Seam ripper

Fig. 7.   Tracing wheel

Have plenty of good-quality pins; a seam ripper (Fig. 6); and a package of tailor's chalk, dressmaker's tracing paper, and a tracing wheel (Fig. 7) for marking guidelines on your cloth.

To complete the list: needles for hand-sewing in sizes 5 to 10 sharps, a thimble, an eighteen-inch ruler, a tape measure, Scotch tape, extra tissue paper, and pencils.

CHAPTER TWO

A Perfect Fit

Before you go to the store to buy a pants pattern, you should decide what is the best size pattern for you.

There are several different categories of pattern sizes, so the first thing to do is to find out which one is the nearest to your figure type. Complete size charts are printed in the back of large pattern catalogues and also in the small home catalogues.

The kinds of patterns most suited to girls and young women are called:

Girls, Chubbies, Young Junior/Teen, Junior, Junior Petite, or *Misses.* If you are very large for your age, or overweight, you may want to consider *Women's* or *Half-size* patterns.

All these possibilities may seem very confusing, but when you learn to take your measurements you will find that one type is the best for you, and you can ignore the others. Here's how you decide:

Girls. The best type for young girls whose figures have not matured at all, with flat hips and no bust development.

Chubbies. Similar to *Girls,* but over average weight for the age.

Young Junior/Teen. Teen-age girls, just beginning to develop some curves in the hips and bust, about 5'1" to 5'3" tall.

The other pattern types are for mature figures. It will be helpful to take your back waist length measurement. Even though this does not actually enter into the pants pattern, it is a guide to the over-all proportions of the body.

You will need help in taking this measurement. Tie a string snugly around your waist, rolling it down to the smallest part of the waist. Bend your head slightly forward, and have someone measure from the prominent bone at the back of the neck down to the string (Fig. 8).

If the back waist length measures between 14" and 15¼", and you are between 5' and 5'1" tall, the *Junior Petite* patterns are for you.

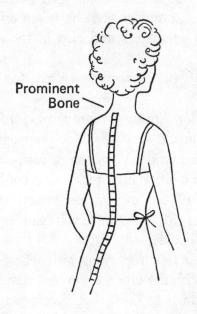

Prominent
Bone

Fig. 8.   Measuring back waist length

For a slightly taller figure, 5′4″ to 5′5″, with a back waist length from 15″ to 16¼″, *Junior* is the best size.

A girl 5′5″ or over, with a back waist length of 15½″ to 17¼″, will wear a *Misses* size.

For the heavier figure, and a short girl, with back waist length between 15″ and 16¼″, and with a waist large in proportion to hips, the *Half-size* pattern is best.

Taller, heavier girls can use a *Women's* pattern.

Now that you have decided what type of pattern to buy, you will need to take more measurements to determine the *exact size*. The *hip* and *waist* measurements will determine this.

Measure over your underwear or close-fitting garments, pulling the tape measure so it is just a snug fit, around the smallest part of the waist, and the largest part of the hips, wherever that may be (Fig. 9).

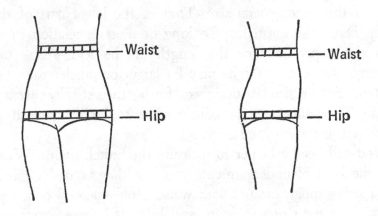

Fig. 9.   Measuring waist and hips

Look at the measurements on the chart, under the type of pattern you have chosen, and find the nearest waist measurement. Then check to see if the corresponding hip measurement is the same as yours.

For example, if you are a Misses size, and your waist is 25″, the corresponding hip size is 34½″. But your hips measure 36″, so you should buy the next larger size pattern, which has a 26½″ waist. Always go by the hip measurement, because it is easier to make the waist smaller than to enlarge the hips on the pattern.

Now you are ready to buy your pattern. If you are a beginner, choose something very simple: two pieces (front and back), with either a plain waistband or elastic casing. Don't get involved with pockets, yokes, or trimmings at this point.

Before you cut out your pattern, you need to take a few more measurements. This may seem like a lot of trouble, but it will simplify things in the long run. Wherever the body has moving joints, there are more difficulties in fitting. (The other major fitting problem is a set-in sleeve, for the same reasons.) Write down all these measurements.

The length of the crotch varies a great deal even among girls of the same general size. That is, the lower part of the body, below the waist, may be long or short in relation to either the upper body or the length of the legs. Also your tummy, buttocks, or thighs may be larger or smaller than the pattern size, which is designed for a theoretically average figure. The pants must be comfortable, too, when you sit or walk, not just when you stand still.

You will need a helper to measure the crotch depth. Wearing the kind of undergarments you would wear under pants, tie a string snugly around your waist. Hold one end of a tape measure at the string in front, and bring it between your legs and up to the string in back (Fig. 10). Your friend will find the correct measurement in back.

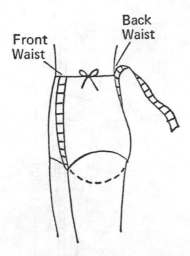

Fig. 10.   Measuring crotch depth

Then measure from the front of the string to the point where the inside leg seam of the pants would start. Write down the total crotch measurement, subtract the front length from the total, and this will give you the back length.

For example, the total is 28″, and the front is 13¼″, so the back will be 14¾″. Add an extra ¾″ to both front and back, for wearing ease.

Next, measure around the heaviest part of one thigh, and find the total pants length by measuring down the side from the waist to the point where you want the hem to be (Fig. 11).

Now you are ready to get out your pattern and see how your measurements compare.

First, the *crotch depth.* Measure the front and back crotch length of the pattern, between the seam lines (Fig. 12).

If these are not the same as your own measurements (including the ¾″ ease), the pattern must be changed. You will see a line across the upper part of the back pattern piece with the caption "Lengthen or shorten here" (Fig. 13). Let

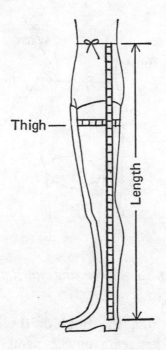

Thigh—

Length

Fig. 11.   *Measuring thigh and total length*

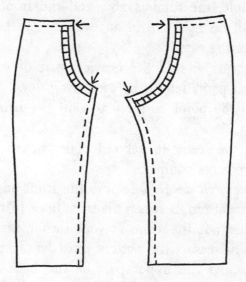

Fig. 12.   *Measuring crotch length of pattern*

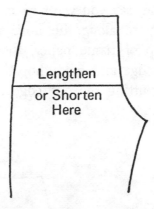

Fig. 13.   Line for lengthening or shortening pattern

us say, for example, that you decide both the front and back should be made 1″ shorter. Draw a pencil line 1″ above the first line, fold the pattern along the shortening line, bring it up to meet the pencil line, and tape or pin it in place (Fig. 14).

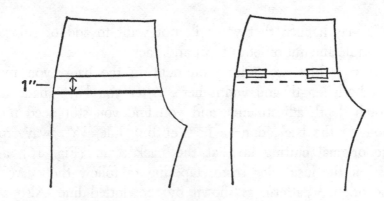

Fig. 14.   Shortening crotch of pattern

On the other hand, say you want to make the pattern ½″ longer. Cut the pattern along the horizontal line, tape one part of it to a strip of tissue paper, then draw a line ½″ away from the cut edge and tape the other part of the pattern to the tissue, putting the cut edge right on the pencil line (Fig. 15).

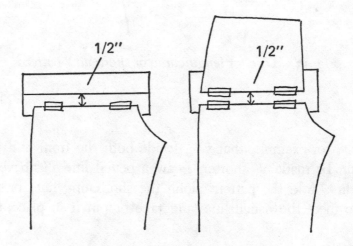

Fig. 15.   *Lengthening crotch of pattern*

It may happen that you will not want to add or subtract the same amount on both front and back.

If your hips are quite prominent in the back, you must add both length and width here. *After* you have made any crotch depth adjustments, and you find you still need more room in the back, draw a new cutting line, ½″ away from the original cutting line, at the back seam (Fig. 16) and also at the inside leg seam, tapering to follow the curve of the original pattern, as shown by the dotted line. Also add ½″ at the top, and taper it toward the side seam. If there is

not enough room for this on the pattern, tape on extra strips of tissue.

Do not try to add on more than ½″ here. If this is not enough, you should have a larger pattern.

On the other hand, if you are rather flat in the back, and the back crotch depth of the pattern is longer than your own measurement (while the front is just right), the pattern should be shortened at the center back. At the horizontal line, take up a tuck at the center back, as deep as necessary, and taper it to nothing at the side seam.

This will slightly distort the shape of the back and side seams, so redraw the seams like the dotted line in Fig. 17, taking off about ¼″ at the center back, adding the same at the side, and tapering both lines down to the ends of the tuck.

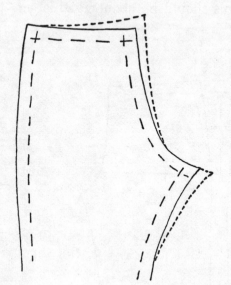

Fig. 16. *Enlarging back of pattern*

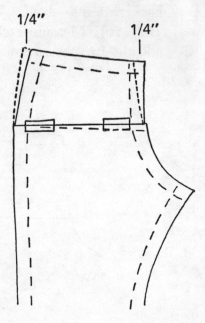

1/4″   1/4″

Fig. 17. *Shortening center back of pattern*

Waist. If your waist is small in proportion to your hip size, you must draw new cutting lines at both side seams of the pattern, as in Fig. 18. To find out how much to subtract, take the difference between your waist and the pattern waist, as listed on the size chart, and divide by 4. (You are going to alter the right and left front and right and left back, which adds up to 4.)

For example, your waist is 1″ smaller than the pattern. Divide by 4, and you have ¼″ to be taken off each side (each pattern piece of course, is one half of the front or back). Measure in ¼″ at the top, and taper the new side seam down to nothing at a point 7″ below the waist.

If your waist is larger than the pattern, you will do the same thing in reverse. Add on the desired amount at both side seams (Fig. 19), and taper down to nothing.

Thigh width. Draw a straight line across both front and back patterns, about 3″ below the end of the crotch seam (Fig. 20). Measure each piece between the seam lines, and add the two measurements. This should be about 2½″ larger

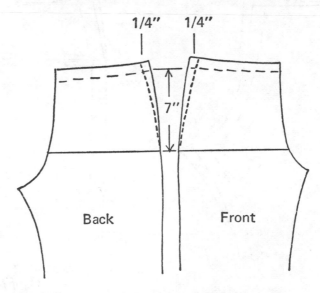

Fig. 18.   Making waist of pattern smaller

than your own thigh, to allow for ease in walking and sitting. If you have less than 2½″ ease, you should widen the legs, and if there is more than 2½″, the legs should be made narrower.

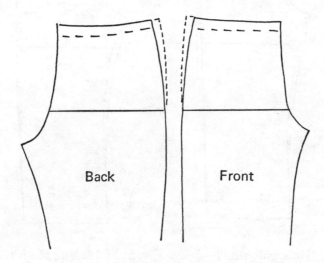

Fig. 19.   *Enlarging waist of pattern*

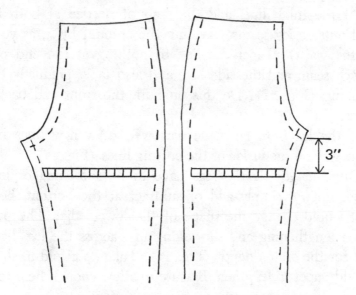

Fig. 20.   *Measuring thigh width of pattern*

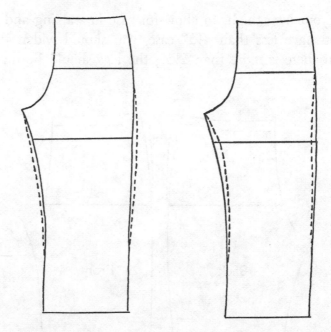

Fig. 21.   *Enlarging thigh*   Fig. 22.   *Making thigh narrower*

At the thigh line, add the amount needed at both inside and outside leg seams (dividing the amount by 4, as you did at the waist). Taper the line to nothing at the end of the crotch seam and the side hip, and also taper gradually to the hemline (Fig. 21). Do this on both the front and back patterns.

If the leg is to be made narrower, draw new lines in the same way on the *inside* of the cutting lines (Fig. 22).

Pants length. If the legs have to be shortened or lengthened, do not simply add or subtract at the bottom, because that would change the shape of the lower edge. The pattern has a lengthening and shortening line across the leg, like the one for the crotch depth (Fig. 23). Take up a fold to shorten, or add paper to lengthen. Be sure to allow enough hem to turn up.

Now you are ready to cut out your pants. If you did not have to make any serious changes in the pattern, it should be safe to go ahead with your good material.

However, if you have made a lot of changes, it is a good idea to try out your pattern in scrap material first. It is worth taking a little extra time to do this because you will not take a chance on ruining your good fabric, and you will end up with a perfectly fitting pattern that you can work from in the future. The same fitting changes can be transferred to any other pants pattern, so you will not have to do any more tedious fitting.

Old sheets are fine to use for trial patterns. If you don't have any, buy the least expensive cotton remnants you can find. (It doesn't matter how ugly they are!)

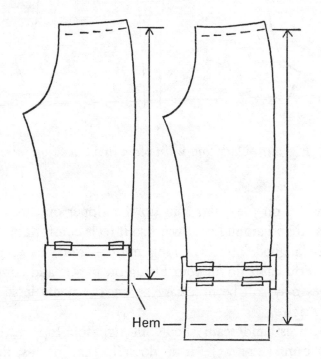

Hem

Fig. 23. Shortening or lengthening pants

Cut out the pants front and back pieces, and the waistband, if any. Use tracing paper to transfer the dart lines and also the waist seam and waistband seam lines (Fig. 24). Put the pieces together, following the directions in Chapter Three or Four. Use a long machine basting stitch, and don't bother about details like zippers and pockets. Fold the waistband in half lengthwise and press, but leave it separate.

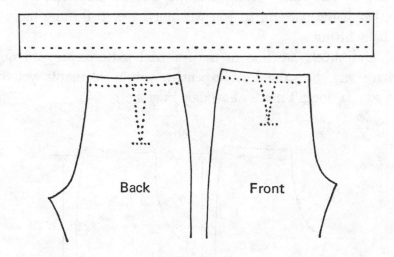

Fig. 24.   Darts and waist seam line traced on fabric

Now try on the pants, pin up the zipper opening, and pin the waistband around your waist so it feels comfortable.

Take a good look in a long mirror—front, back, and side views. You can't do all your fitting on paper, and some minor changes may still be necessary before the pants look and feel exactly right.

The waistband seam should fit right on top of the pants waist seam (Fig. 25); if it doesn't, that means the pants must be lengthened or shortened to fit.

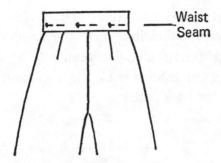

Fig. 25.   Pinning waistband to pants

A common problem for a slim-hipped figure is to have the back waist of the pants fit too high above the natural waist (Fig. 26). In this case the pants will also look baggy in the seat (Fig. 27).

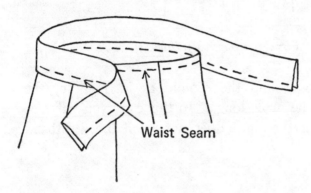

Fig. 26.   Back of pants too high above waist

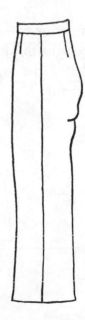

Fig. 27.   Pants too long in back

Pin a horizontal tuck across the back of the pants, 3" or 4" below the waist, adjusting until the back fits smoothly, tapering the tuck toward the side seams (Fig. 28). Measure how much you have taken up in the tuck and take up the same amount of the back pattern.

Fig. 28.   Pinning up extra fullness in back

If wrinkles form around the crotch, as in Fig. 29, the crotch depth must be made longer. In this case, you will also find that the top of the pants does not reach the waistband (Fig. 30).

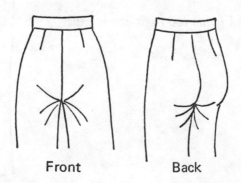

Front   Back

Fig. 29.   Too-short crotch causes wrinkles

Fig. 30.   *Too-short crotch does not reach waistband*

If both the front and back are too short, add an equal amount to both the front and back of the pattern (as in Fig. 15).

If only one part needs to be longer, cut across the horizontal line on the pattern, tape the lower part to a strip of paper, and measure the extra length needed at the crotch seam. Draw a line tapering to nothing at the side seam (Fig. 31). Tape the upper part of the pattern. Extend the waistline half the amount added to the length, and draw a line tapering to nothing at the horizontal slash (dotted line in Fig. 31).

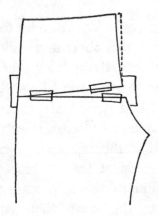

Fig. 31.   *Lengthening back or front crotch of pattern*

Look at your side seams. You may want to take them in or let them out a little for a more flattering fit. The curve of the hip can vary a great deal, even in girls of the same general size, so you have to get the exact shape by pinning it on your own figure (or have a friend do it, if possible) (Fig. 32).

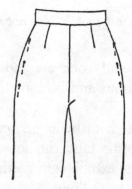

Fig. 32.   Pinning in side seams at hip

The shape of the pants legs may be too wide to suit you, especially if you are rather short and wide-hipped. Many patterns have a rather wide, straight leg that falls straight to the hem from the widest part of the hip, without tapering at the knee (Fig. 33). (This is typical of patterns for home sewing, while many ready-made pants have a more tapered leg.)

You can see that if the hip area is extra wide, then the pants will be very wide at the bottom (Fig. 34), which is most unflattering. Pin in the side seam so it fits smoothly, but easily, down to the knee, then let it continue in a straight line to the hem.

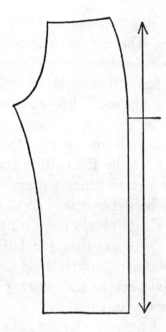

Fig. 33.   Pants pattern with straight leg

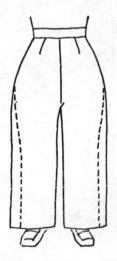

Fig. 34. Making pant legs narrower

Girls with very slim legs may find that the pants are baggy around the thighs. The leg seams should be taken in more, both inside and outside seams, as in Fig. 22.

If you have a figure that looks attractive in pants that fit very closely at the hip and thigh, you should look for a pattern designed to fit this way. Many patterns are meant to hang straight down from the back of the hips, as in Fig. 35, and you can't get a really form-fitting style with this type of pattern. Look for a closer-fitting pattern. A style with a seam running down the back is especially good (Fig. 36).

Make a final check of all the fitting details. The waist should be just a bit larger than the finished waistband. Try sitting down to be sure the crotch is not too tight.

Transfer any changes to the paper pattern, and you are ready to cut and sew your pants.

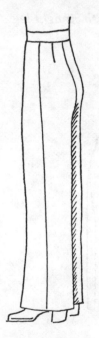

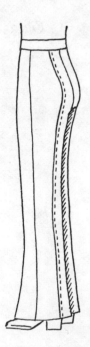

Fig. 35.   Pants hanging
straight in back

Fig. 36.   Pants with
fitted back seam

CHAPTER THREE

The Simplest Basic Pants

The simplest pants you can make are a two-piece pattern with an elastic waist and no zipper, pockets, or trim.

Even the youngest beginning sewer can learn to make these, and they are very suitable for younger girls who don't yet have a well-defined waistline. They don't slide down over the hips, and the elastic expands enough to fit a rapidly growing girl.

For anyone, they are exceptionally comfortable, as they will not bind at the waist.

Knit materials are most suitable to use with an elastic waist pattern, because some of the comfortable fit comes from the built-in stretch of the fabric, so some of the bulk can be eliminated from the waist.

There are some disadvantages to this style. If your waist is quite small in proportion to your hips, there will be a lot of extra material around the waist, because the pants waist must be made wide enough to slip over the fullest part of the hips. The extra fabric will gather up around the waist, as in Fig. 37. For this type of figure, it is better to use a pattern that has a zipper in addition to the elastic, so the waist can be tapered in at the sides (Fig. 38).

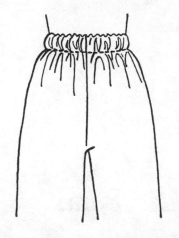

Fig. 37.   *Extra gathers around
small waist*

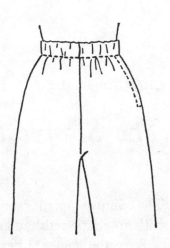

Fig. 38.   *Pants with elastic
plus zipper*

Another disadvantage is that this style does not look very attractive with a tucked-in blouse. If you like to wear over-blouses or tunics, however, the elastic waist is perfect, as it does not show.

Now you have chosen your pattern, made any necessary alterations to it, and are ready to cut out the pants.

First, look at the pattern layout chart to find out which layout you are going to use. Different layouts will be shown, depending on the width of the material, the size of the pattern, and whether the material has a nap or one-way design.

Most cottons are 45″ wide, and you should find a layout something like Fig. 39. You will notice that the two narrow ends of the pattern pieces are dovetailed together, which saves a bit of yardage.

Selvages

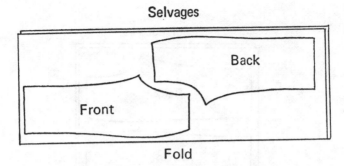

Fold

Fig. 39.   Pattern layout on 45″ fabric

If the fabric has a nap (as explained in Chapter One, about corduroy) or a design running all one way (Fig. 40), you must lay out the pieces as in Fig. 41. You can see that this requires a little more material.

Fig. 40.   Fabric with one-way design

Selvages

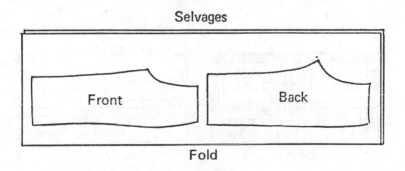

Fold

Fig. 41.   Pattern layout for one-way fabric

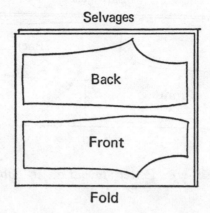

Selvages

Back

Front

Fold

Fig. 42.   Pattern layout for 58″ or 60″ fabric

If the fabric is 58″ to 60″ wide, as in most knits and wools, the two pattern pieces can probably be laid side by side, as in Fig. 42.

For a pants layout, the fabric must be carefully folded *lengthwise*, bringing the two selvages together. The selvage is the finished lengthwise edge of the cloth. On some knits it may be hard to see the selvage, but you will be able to pick out a line of small dots, showing where the edges of the fabric were attached to the machine (Fig. 43).

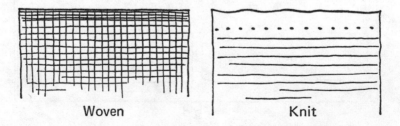

Woven

Knit

Fig. 43.   Selvage of woven and knit fabrics

Fold the material, bringing the two selvages evenly together, and smooth out any wrinkles. Pin the edges if the fabric is slippery. Be sure that the cut ends line up also. If they have not been cut evenly, you can pull a crosswise thread of woven material, then cut off along the pulled line (Fig. 44). You can't pull a thread on a knit, but you can usually find a crosswise line in the pattern and trim it evenly (Fig. 45).

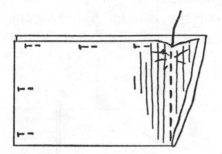

Fig. 44.   *Pulling thread of woven fabric*

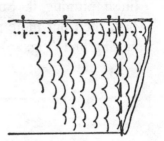

Fig. 45.   *Trimming knit fabric on crosswise line*

On each pattern piece you will see a lengthwise line, with an arrow at each end, labeled "Place on lengthwise grain of fabric." This line is on the part of the pattern that hangs straight down the front or back of the body, and if it is not laid straight on the fabric, the garment will appear twisted to one side. Cutting pieces according to the straight grain is one of the most important rules you will ever learn in constructing clothing. If this step is done wrong, it doesn't matter how well you sew—the garment will never look right.

Here is the way you determine that your pattern is laid on the straight grain:

For the grain line to be parallel to the lengthwise threads of the fabric, it must be an even distance from either the selvages or the long lengthwise fold (measure from whichever is closer).

Place the pattern piece so it looks as straight as possible, pin it to the fabric at one end of the grain line, and measure this distance from the edge. Then check the other end of the line to see if it is the same distance from the edge. If it is not, slide the pattern up or down until it is correct, and put another pin at that end of the line (Fig. 46).

Now the pattern is safely anchored in place, and you can finish pinning it. Smooth out the pattern, pin the corners first, then put more pins about 5″ or 6″ apart, just inside the cutting line (Fig. 47).

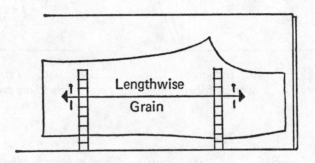

Fig. 46. Laying out pattern on straight grain

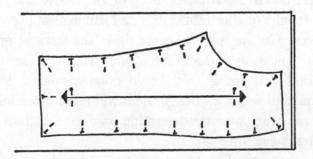

Fig. 47. Pinning pattern

Pin all the pieces before you start cutting, then with your large shears cut through the center of the heavy cutting line, using long, smooth strokes. When you come to the little notches on the cutting line, cut *outward* around them (Fig. 48). If you cut *into* the seam allowance you might make too large a hole in the seam, especially if your hand is not too steady.

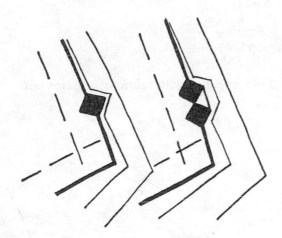

Fig. 48.   Cutting notches

If you do not have much experience in stitching, you may want to mark the curved crotch seam with a guide line. Curved seams are a little hard to follow at first.

Use dressmaker's tracing paper of a contrasting color, and place two sheets of it facing the two *wrong* sides of the cloth. If your fabric is folded *wrong* side out, the paper will be on the top and bottom, with the coated sides facing each other, and the pattern on top (Fig. 49).

If the fabric is folded *right* side out, place two sheets of paper between the two layers, with the coated sides facing away from each other (Fig. 50).

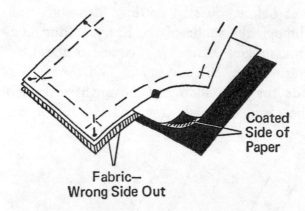

Fig. 49.   *Tracing paper, with fabric wrong side out*

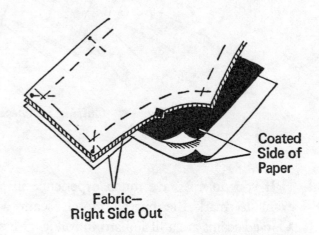

Fig. 50.   *Tracing paper, with fabric right side out*

Trace over the dotted seam line on the pattern with a tracing wheel, using a good firm pressure (Fig. 51). Remove the pattern and tracing paper. If the marking does not show up clearly enough, you can mark over it with chalk.

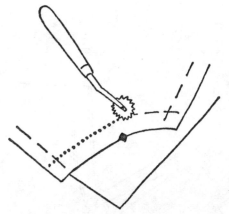

Fig. 51.   Marking with tracing wheel

Now you are ready to begin stitching. Thread your sewing machine, and test the stitching on two layers of your leftover fabric, to see if it looks just right. The stitch length should be set at 10 or 12 to the inch, and the tension disc should be adjusted if necessary so the stitching looks even and smooth.

Start with the front of the pants. Place the two fronts with the *right* sides together, edges even and notches together, and pin the crotch seam with pins at right angles to the edge (Fig. 52). Stitch the seam from bottom to top, following the line that you marked. Back-tack with 3 or 4 stitches at each end. Stitch over the seam a second time, for extra strength (Fig. 53).

Clip the curved part of the seam, almost up to the stitching, using the tips of your scissors (Fig. 53). This is done so that the seam can be pressed open. Press it over a special pressing cushion, if you have one, or over a tightly rolled heavy towel (Fig. 54). It is hard to press a curved seam over a flat surface.

Always press every seam after you stitch it, so that it will lie flat and be all ready to be joined to the next seam.

Pin, stitch, clip, and press the back crotch seam in the same way.

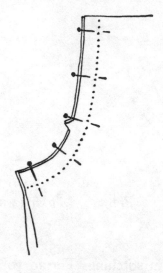

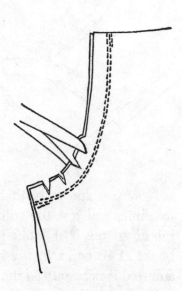

Fig. 52.   *Pinning and
stitching crotch seam*

Fig. 53.   *Restitching and
clipping crotch seam*

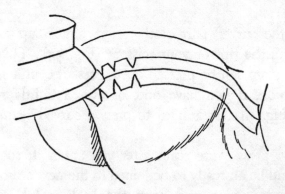

Fig. 54.   *Pressing crotch seam*

Now place the front and back of the pants with the right sides together, and pin both side seams. Match the notches and top and bottom edges, then add more pins, 4″ or 5″ apart (Fig. 55).

You will notice that the back of the pants is wider than the front. Don't worry—it is supposed to be, because *you* are wider in back. Just see that the *seam edges* come evenly together, and keep the rest of the material out of the way.

Stitch each side from *bottom* to *top*. Be sure to take up the full ⅝″ seam allowance. This is standard on all patterns, and if you take up more or less, the garment will not fit the same.

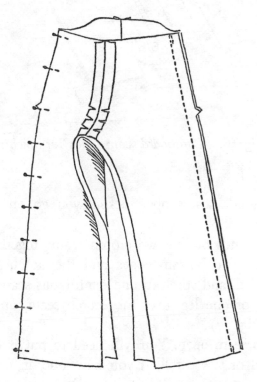

Fig. 55.   Pinning and stitching side seams

If your sewing machine does not have a seam guide or marking, you can make one. Cut a strip of cardboard and Scotch-tape it exactly ⅝″ to the right of the needle hole (Fig. 56). By guiding the edge of the cloth along the cardboard, you will achieve a perfectly even seam width.

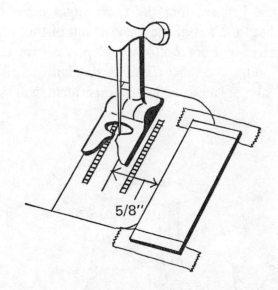

Fig. 56.   *Cardboard seam guide for machine*

Press the side seams open before you go on to the next step.

Bring the ends of the two crotch seams together and pin, then pin the two bottom edges and the notches, add more pins as needed, and stitch in one continuous seam, starting at the bottom of one leg, over the crotch seam, and down the other leg (Fig. 57).

Press this seam open. You will need to put it over a small sleeve board or sleeve roll, if you have one, in order to work on such a narrow area. You can make a very good pressing tool. Roll up a large magazine, roll a terry towel over it, and fasten the ends with rubber bands (Fig. 58). This is also handy for pressing sleeves or any small area.

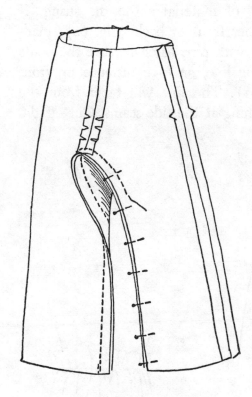

Fig. 57.   *Stitching inside leg seams*

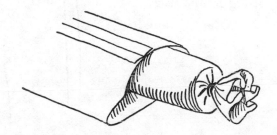

Fig. 58.   *Pressing roll made from a magazine*

Now turn the pants right side out, and try them on. Without the elastic, you will not be able to see how the waist fits, so tie a string snugly around your waist and pull the top of the pants under it, adjusting the fullness evenly (Fig. 59). There should be about 1″ of material above the string. If there is extra length in either front or back (Fig. 60), mark along the line of the string with pins or chalk, take the pants off, and mark a new cutting line, an even distance up from the waist marking (Fig. 61). The line will taper from the center back or front to nothing at the side seams. Cut off the extra material.

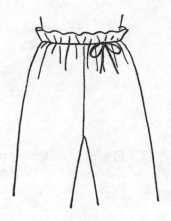

Fig. 59. Fitting pants with string around waist

Fig. 60. Extra length above string

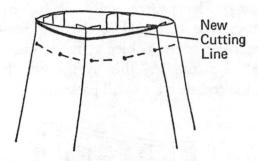

New
Cutting
Line

Fig. 61.   Marking new cutting line

If you are using a knit fabric, you may be able to take in the side seams at the waist, tapering toward the hips (Fig. 62). This will eliminate some of the extra fullness that would be gathered up around the elastic. Pin in the waist and see if the extra stretch will allow the waist to slide easily over your hips. Making the waist as small as possible gives a smoother fit.

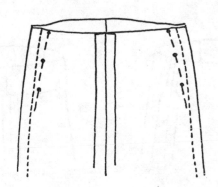

Fig. 62.   Pinning extra fullness out of waist

Elastic casing. The pattern will call for either 1"- or ¾"-wide elastic. The best kind is the new non-roll elastic, which has crosswise ridges to keep it from twisting and folding (Fig. 63). You can buy this by the yard from a large roll, at much less cost than the small packages.

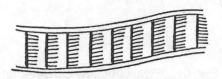

Fig. 63.   Non-roll elastic

Trim some of the seam allowance fom the upper 2" of the pants seams (Fig. 64). This will make it easier for the elastic to slide through.

Fold down the top of the pants to the inside, the width shown on the pattern. Measure the width in several places and pin (Fig. 65). If you are using a knit material, the raw edge does not have to be finished, because it does not fray.

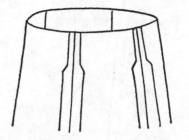

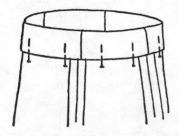

Fig. 64.   Upper seam   allowance trimmed

Fig. 65.   Turning down top of   pants for casing

For woven fabrics, press under ¼″ along the edge before turning it down (Fig. 66).

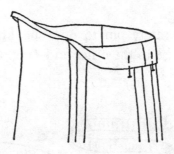

Fig. 66.   Edge of casing pressed under

Test the elastic against the width of the casing. This should be just wide enough for the elastic to slip in easily, and not so wide that it will slide around.

Stitch close to the lower edge of the casing, leaving about 1″ open at the back seam (Fig. 67). Stitch again close to the upper folded edge.

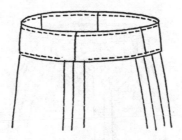

Fig. 67.   Stitching both edges of casing

Measure a piece of elastic around your waist so it just fits snugly without stretching. Allow about 1" overlap. This will have to be adjusted for size after the elastic has been put through the casing.

Attach a large safety pin to one end of the elastic, and a second pin crosswise to the other end (Fig. 68).

Fig. 68.   Safety pins attached to elastic

Start the pin through the back opening, and work it all the way through until it comes out again (Fig. 69). Keep pulling the elastic all the way through so the cloth does not all bunch up at one end. Lap the ends of the elastic, and pin (Fig. 70). Slip it back into the casing, try on the pants, and adjust the length of the elastic so it feels comfortable.

Fig. 69.   Elastic pulled through casing

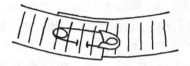

Fig. 70. Pinning lapped ends of elastic

Cut off any excess (1″ overlap is enough), and sew the
ends together with several rows of stitching, back and forth
across the elastic (Fig. 71), or overcast both edges by hand
(Fig. 72). Finally, stitch up the rest of the back opening of
the casing.

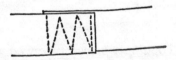

Fig. 71.   Machine-stitched elastic

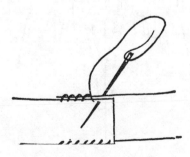

Fig. 72.   Sewing elastic by hand

If you decided to use a zipper as well as elastic, insert it in the back opening before sewing the casing, following the directions in Chapter Four for a centered zipper.

Place the top of the zipper just below where the bottom edge of the elastic will come (Fig. 73). Then turn down and stitch the casing. The elastic goes in through the open end above the zipper and comes out the opposite end (Fig. 74).

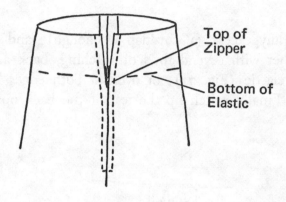

Fig. 73.   Top of zipper placed below edge of elastic

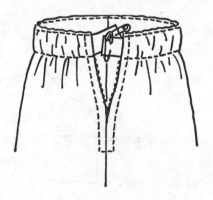

Fig. 74.   Inserting elastic above zipper

Adjust the length, and stitch across both ends through all layers, to hold the elastic in place (Fig. 75). Trim off the excess elastic, and fasten the top with a hook and eye.

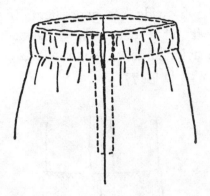

Fig. 75. Stitching ends of elastic

Try on the pants to decide how much hem to turn up at the bottom. The ideal length is just to the point where the heel of the shoe joins the upper shoe (Fig. 76), so the pants should be tried on with the shoes that will be worn with them.

Turn up the back of one pant leg so it looks right with the shoes, then turn up and pin the same width of hem all

Fig. 76. Correct pants length

around both legs. The front of the pants will just cover the instep, without wrinkling.

Except for very casual jeans, pants should always be finished with a hand-sewn hem, as invisible as possible.

About 2" or 2½" wide is a good hem. If you have extra, trim some of it off evenly. The edge should be neatly finished. For heavier knits or wools a zigzag stitch close to the edge works well (Fig. 77).

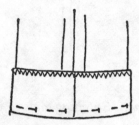

Fig. 77.   Zigzag finish on hem

Here is the best type of hem for heavy fabrics: instead of sewing *over* the hem edge, roll it back about ¼", holding it with your thumb, while you take small stitches, first on the pants, then on the hem (Fig. 78). Sewing a little way down from the hem edge prevents a ridge from showing on the right side.

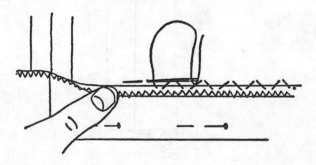

Fig. 78.   Sewing an invisible hem

For lighter-weight fabrics or those that fray easily, stitch plain or lace seam binding along the edge, and slip-stitch the hem, as in Fig. 79. For a right-handed person, hold the hem edge of the pants over your left hand, as shown, and sew from *right* to *left*. This makes a stitch that is concealed under the hem edge.

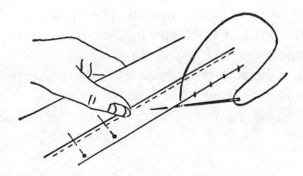

Fig. 79. Slip-stitching hem with seam binding

Pressing. First press the hems, along the folded edge only, to prevent the hem edge from showing a ridge.

To crease the legs, find the correct position of the creases by bringing the inside and outside leg seams together, one leg at a time. Pin the seams together, and spread the pant leg flat on the ironing board (Fig. 80). Cover the fabric with a

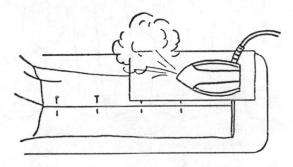

Fig. 80. Creasing pant legs

cotton press cloth, to prevent marks from the iron, and steam-press each crease as far up to the top of the pants as you can reach, without shifting the position of the pant leg. (Use a damp cloth over a dry press cloth if you do not have a steam iron.)

Now lift up the pants and fold and press each crease the rest of the way up to the waist. The creases should follow the straight grain of the material. The creases go all the way up to the waist in front, and in the back they stop 4" or 5" below the waist and appear to slant in toward the center (Fig. 81). Be sure that the ends of the creases are an even distance from the center front and back seams.

If you like, the *front* creases may be topstitched close to the edge.

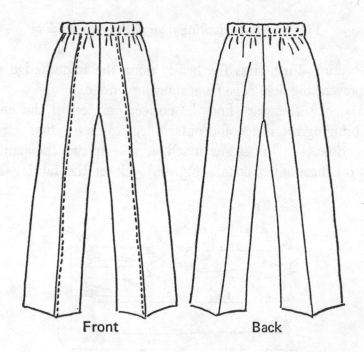

Front   Back

Fig. 81. Front and back creases

CHAPTER FOUR

Waistbands and Zippers

After you have acquired confidence in making the basic elastic-waist pants, you will want to branch out into making more fitted and tailored styles. The kind of good wool pants that you want to wear with tailored blazers and tucked-in shirts should be smoothly fitted, with darts, zipper, and waistband. Pockets and cuffs are extra touches that you can easily add after you have learned the basic method.

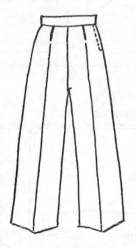

Fig. 82. Basic pants pattern with waistband

Choose a simple pattern (with whatever leg style you prefer: narrow, wide, or bell-bottomed). There will be either one or two darts on each side of the front and back, and a plain waistband at the natural waist position. The zipper can be put into any seam—front, back, or side—regardless of where the pattern directions place it (Fig. 82).

The pattern is laid out and cut in the same way as for the pants in Chapter Three, with the addition of a waistband. This is cut from a single layer of material and can be on either the lengthwise or the crosswise grain of the fabric, depending on where you have room for it (Fig. 83).

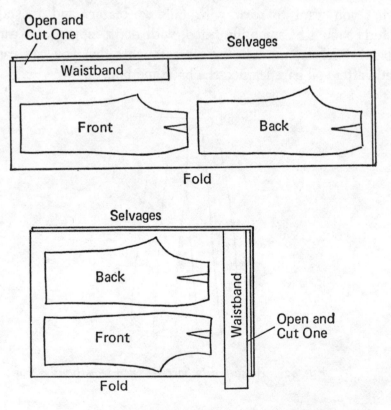

Fig. 83.   Two pattern layouts, with waistband

Before you remove the pattern, the dart lines must be marked. Use tracing paper and wheel for lightweight fabrics. Mark along both dotted lines, and along the center line, and make a short mark across the point (Fig. 84).

If you are using a fairly heavy wool, the tracing will probably not show up clearly, and you will have to use another method.

Be sure the material is folded *wrong* side out before you lay out and cut the pattern. Push a pin straight through each of the dots on the dart marking, through all layers, so it comes out on the underside (Fig. 85). Make a chalk mark at each pin on the underside, then pull the pattern carefully away from the pins and mark the top side the same way (Fig. 86).

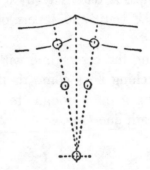

Fig. 84.   *Marking dart lines*

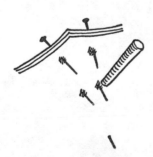

Fig. 85.   *Marking dart with pins—under side*

Fig. 86.   *Marking dart with pins—top side*

There are different ways of putting together the three main sets of seams in pants. In this chapter you are going to learn a different method from the one you used in Chapter Three. The order of seams is: (1) inside leg seams; (2) entire crotch seam; (3) outside leg seams.

This method is generally used in professional tailoring because it gives a smoother fit and helps to eliminate wrinkling at the crotch seam.

Sewing the darts. There is a particular technique to this that you should practice until you can do it smoothly, because there are darts in most things that you sew.

A dart is a device for fitting and shaping an area, such as the waist, that is smaller than an adjoining part of the body —in this case, the hips. A dart is really a partial seam. It begins as a seam at the waist and tapers off to nothing at its end.

Fold the dart along the center line with the right sides in. Be sure the two stitching lines come right together. You can check this by putting a pin through, to see if it comes out right on the underneath line (Fig. 87).

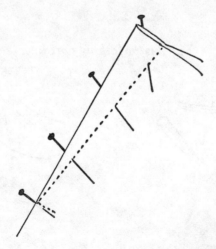

Fig. 87.   Bringing dart stitching lines together

Put pins in the dart at right angles to the stitching line, with the last pin marking the point. If the dart has been marked with dots of chalk, you can draw a line to connect them with a ruler and chalk (Fig. 88).

Stitch the dart, starting at the wide end. Backstitch, and continue to the pointed end. Stitch slowly here, so you can be sure to make a very fine point. The last two or three stitches should be almost on the edge of the cloth, then run right off the end, without trying to backstitch (Fig. 89). Tie the ends in a double knot and trim to ½".

This makes a smooth, rounded end to the dart, so it will lie flat when it is pressed.

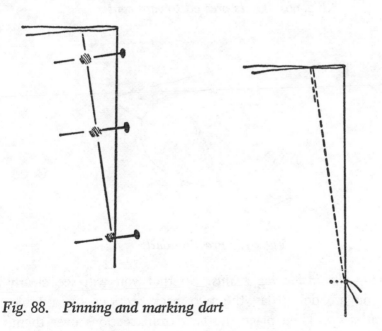

Fig. 88. *Pinning and marking dart*

Fig. 89. *Dart correctly stitched*

Darts are always pressed *toward* the center of the garment (Fig. 90). Lay the dart over your pressing cushion, wrong side up, so there are no bubbles around the end, and steam-press (Fig. 91).

Center Front

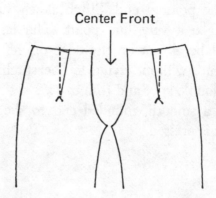

Fig. 90.   *Darts pressed toward center*

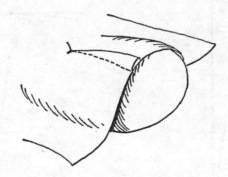

Fig. 91.   *Pressing darts*

Sewing the inside leg seams. So that you will see clearly what you are doing, lay the two back sections on a table, *right sides up.* Then place the two front sections over them, with the *right sides down* (Fig. 92). Pin the top and bottom corners and the notches.

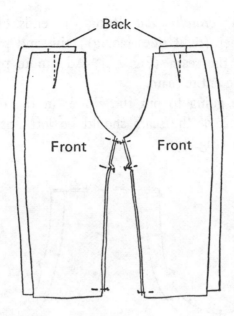

Fig. 92. Pinning inside leg seams

You will notice that the front and back edges are not ex-actly the same shape. Usually the back edge of the seam is to be stretched to fit between the notch and the upper corner (Fig. 93). This is meant to ensure a smoother fit in the back.

Pin the rest of the seam and stitch each leg seam from *bottom* to *top*, and press them open.

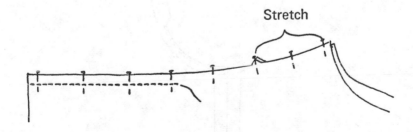

Fig. 93. Stretching back edge of leg seam

Sewing the crotch seam. Bring the ends of the two leg seams together (right sides facing), pin, and pin the notches and ends of the seam (Fig. 94). Add more pins as needed, and stitch the entire seam.

If you are going to put the zipper in the center front or back, this part of the seam should be left unstitched for 8″ from the top (Fig. 95).

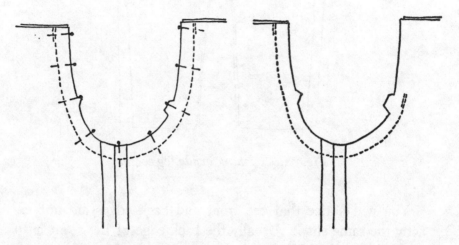

Fig. 94.   *Stitching crotch seam*   Fig. 95.   *Leaving opening for zipper*

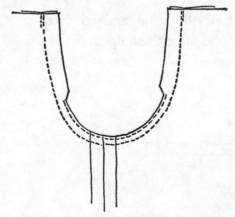

Fig. 96.   *Seam stitched twice and trimmed*

In either case, stitch the seam a second time, ¼" away from the first stitching, over the curved part of the seam— usually between the two sets of notches (Fig. 96). Trim the seam close to the second stitching.

Press the seams open *above* the double stitching. The rest of the seam is not pressed at all. This is the secret of having the pants hang smoothly.

Sewing the side seams. Place the front and back side seams together, right sides together, pin, and stitch from *bottom* to *top* (Fig. 97). Any minor changes in fitting can be done here. Be sure the waist is not too tight. There should be just a little extra fullness to ease into the waistband.

If you are using a side zipper, leave the left side open 8" from the top.

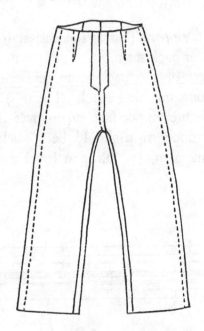

Fig. 97.   *Stitching side seams*

Zippers. There are three basic types of zipper closing that you can make with a standard zipper. (There is also an invisible zipper that you might like to try. It requires a special machine attachment and comes with instructions.)

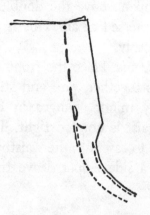

Fig. 98.   Zipper opening basted

The centered zipper. This is the easiest to do, and is used only in the center back seam.

Baste the rest of the back seam, either with small hand basting or a long machine stitch (Fig. 98). Press the seam open and place the zipper face down over it, so it is exactly centered. The zipper stop should be 1″ below the top edge (Fig. 99). Remember, you have to leave room for the waistband.

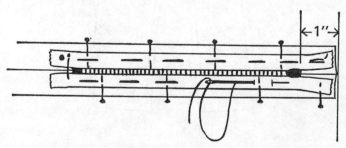

Fig. 99.   Zipper pinned and basted in place

Pin through all thicknesses and hand-baste. Most zippers have a heavy guideline woven through the tape, and if you baste right over this you will have a line of basting on the right side that will show you exactly where to stitch (Fig. 100). Make one stitch just below the bottom of the zipper, so you can see where to stop.

Remove the regular presser foot from the machine, and attach the zipper foot. This is made to fit up to just one side of the needle, so you can get as close to the zipper teeth as you want without riding over it (Fig. 100). For this type of zipper closing, adjust the foot so it is on the *left* side of the needle.

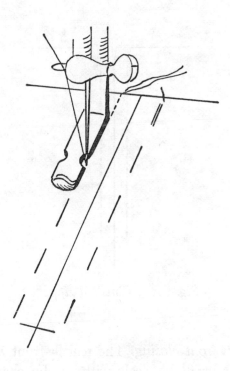

Fig. 100. *Stitching zipper with zipper foot*

Begin stitching at the top left of the zipper, turn a square corner at the bottom, turn again, and stitch up the other side to the top.

Learn to turn a square corner accurately. This is something you will have to do many times while you are sewing. When you reach the corner, leave the needle down *in* the material, lift up the foot, swivel the material around to the correct position, then lower the foot. This prevents the material from shifting, so you get a good sharp corner, with no break in the stitching.

After stitching, remove the bastings from the zipper tape and the center of the seam. If you have been very careful, both sides of the stitching should be an even distance from the center (Fig. 101).

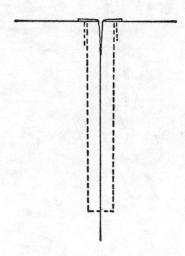

Fig. 101.   Finished zipper

Simplified fly-front closing. The real fly-front zipper is more complicated and will be dealt with in the chapter on jeans (Chapter Five).

If your pattern does not call for a front opening, you will need to make the front seam allowance wider. Measure down 8″ from the top of the pattern, and mark with a dot. This is the bottom stop of the zipper. From a point 1″ below the dot, add ⅜″ to the seam line (Fig. 102). You now have a 1″ seam allowance.

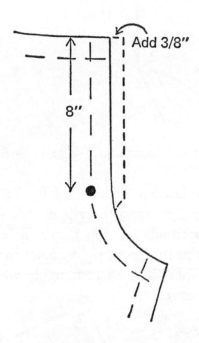

Fig. 102. *Adding width to fly front seam*

Stitch the crotch seam of the pants as far as the dot. The zipper is put in at this point, before the side seams are finished, because it is easier to work with the whole front section spread flat.

On the edge of the front opening that is on your right as you wear the pants, turn under 1″ and press. Turn under and press ¾″ on the left side (Fig. 103).

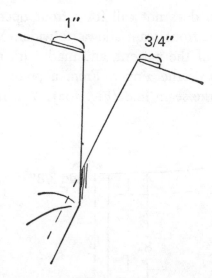

Fig. 103.   Pressing under edges of fly front

Place the zipper face up, under the left edge, with the fold close to the zipper teeth, and the zipper stop just at the bottom end of the opening. The top stop will be 1″ below the upper edge of the pants. Pin at right angles to the edge (Fig. 104). With the zipper foot on your right, stitch close to the folded edge (Fig. 105).

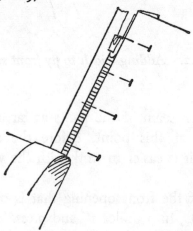

Fig. 104.   Pinning left edge of zipper

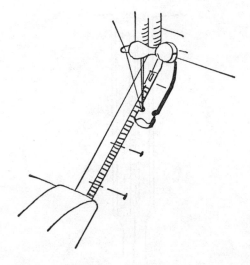

Fig. 105.   Stitching left edge of zipper

Lap the right side ¼″ over the left side, and pin (Fig. 106).

On the wrong side, pin and baste the other zipper tape to the right side, through all thicknesses (Fig. 107).

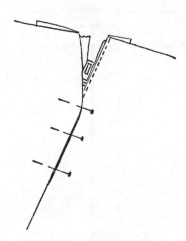

Fig. 106.   Pinning right side over left side of zipper

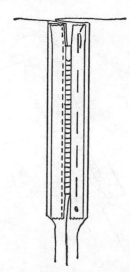

Fig. 107.   Basting right side of zipper

On the right side, mark a curved guideline in basting thread, connecting the lower end of the opening with the other basting. Be sure that the line comes *below* the end of the zipper (Fig. 108).

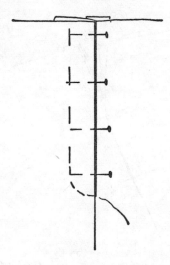

Fig. 108.   Marking guideline with basting

With the *right* side of the pants facing up, and with the zipper foot to the *left* of the needle, stitch from top to bottom, following the basted line, and backstitch firmly at the end (Fig. 109).

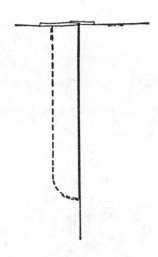

Fig. 109.   Finished fly-front zipper

The left side opening. This looks almost the same as the fly front, but it does not have such a wide overlap. It can be done the same way, but there is another way that is helpful in getting it perfectly straight.

Baste up the side opening with a ⅝″ seam allowance, and press it open. On the wrong side, open out the back seam allowance and pin one tape of the opened zipper face down to the *seam allowance only,* letting the teeth just touch the seam (Fig. 110). With the zipper foot on the *right* side, machine-baste from bottom to top through the guideline (Fig. 111).

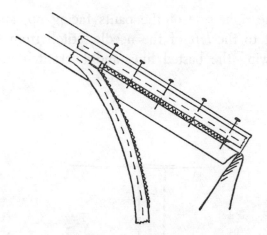

Fig. 110.   Pinning zipper to back seam allowance

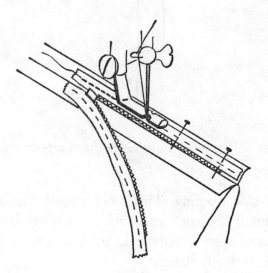

Fig. 111.   Machine-basting zipper tape

Close the zipper and fold it back along the previously basted line. You now have a fold about ⅛″ from the seam line. (You are still working with only the back seam allowance.) Pin the fold in place.

Stitch close to the zipper teeth, with the zipper foot on the left side (Fig. 112).

Fold the zipper back against the *front* seam allowance; pin and baste through *all layers* (Fig. 113).

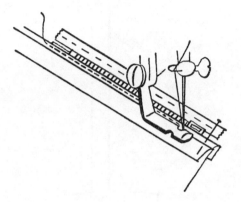

Fig. 112.   *Stitching edge of fold*

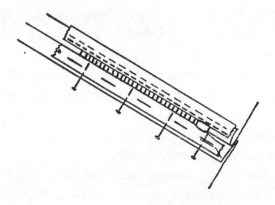

Fig. 113.   *Pinning and basting front edge of zipper*

On the outside, stitch along the basted line and square the stitching at the bottom (Fig. 114). Remove the basting from the side opening.

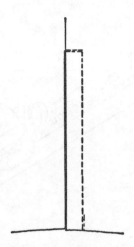

Fig. 114. Finished stitching of side zipper

Waistband. All waistbands need some stiffening to keep them from stretching. Use either a woven or a non-woven interfacing material, of a weight suitable for your fabric. You can also use the fusible kind, but be sure to cut it *lengthwise,* as the crosswise direction is quite stretchy.

You have cut a one-piece waistband, which will be folded in half lengthwise when finished. One half of it will be interfaced.

When using a sewn-in interfacing, cut it a little more than half as wide as the total waistband.

Pin it to the wrong side of the band, with the lower edges together. With a pencil and ruler, draw a line dividing the band in half lengthwise (Fig. 115). The interfacing extends a little beyond the center.

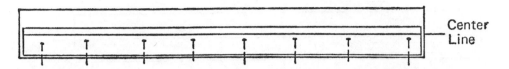

Center
Line

Fig. 115. *Waistband with interfacing and center line*

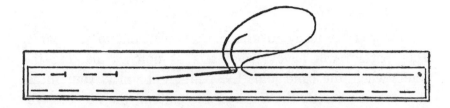

Fig. 116. *Hand-sewing along center line*

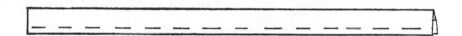

Fig. 117. *Waistband folded in half*

Pin through this line, and sew it with long, loose stitches: a long stitch on the wrong side, and a tiny stitch on the right side (Fig. 116). These stitches will be in the fold after the band is folded and pressed, and will not show.

Machine- or hand-baste the lower edge, ½" from the edge (Fig. 116). Fold the waistband in half lengthwise and crease the fold (Fig. 117).

When using fusible interfacing, cut it so it comes just to the center of the waistband, and eliminate ½" from the other edge (Fig. 118). Fuse it in place with a steam iron, or a dry iron with a damp cloth, following the manufacturer's directions.

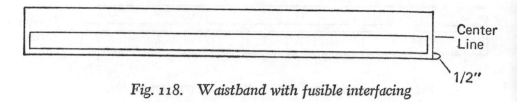

Center
Line

1/2"

Fig. 118. Waistband with fusible interfacing

Now you are ready to attach the waistband to the pants.
Your pattern will have several sets of notches marking the
points where the band joins the pants, but unless your measurements are exactly the same as the pattern, the notches will
not fit together, so ignore them, and do it this way:

With the interfaced side on the outside, fit the band
around your waist, lapping from right to left, and pin so it
feels comfortable. Place one pin ⅝" from the right end of
the band, and another pin directly under it where it laps
over, in the left end (Fig. 119).

The distance between the two pins is the exact length of
the finished band and allows a ⅝" seam at the right end and
an inch or two of overlap at the left.

The procedure for making this band is the same for any
zipper placement: front, back, or side.

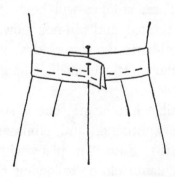

Fig. 119. Lapping and marking ends of waistband

Open out the belt, and measure to find the halfway mark between the two pins (Fig. 120). Divide each section in half again. Now you have a band divided into four equal parts.

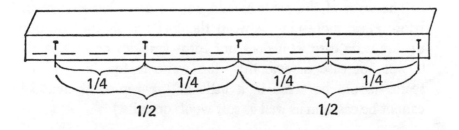

Fig. 120. *Band divided into 4 equal parts*

Mark off the top of the pants into four equal parts also. You will notice that the front waist of the pants is slightly wider than the back, so the side markings will not come exactly at the side seams. Bring the center front and back seams together, lay the pants flat, and mark the fold at both sides (Fig. 121).

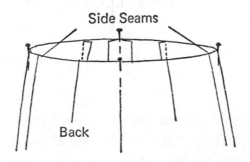

Fig. 121. *Top of pants divided into 4 equal parts*

Attaching the band for a center back zipper. Open the zipper, and pin the right side of the interfaced half of the belt against the right side of the pants. Match the two end pins to the edges of the zipper opening, and pin the other three marked points together (Fig. 122).

The waist of the pants should be just a bit looser than the band. Place more pins between the first set of pins, dividing up the extra ease so it does not form wrinkles or gathers. (If it will not ease in smoothly, the waist is too big and the seams should be taken in a little at the top. Stiff materials cannot be eased in as well as soft wools or knits.)

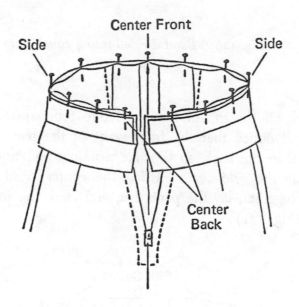

Fig. 122. *Waistband pinned to pants*

Stitch the band with a ⅝″ seam allowance (Fig. 123). Turn the band up and check to see if the two sides of the zipper opening are even at the top (Fig. 124). Sometimes, if you are careless, one side will come out higher than the other.

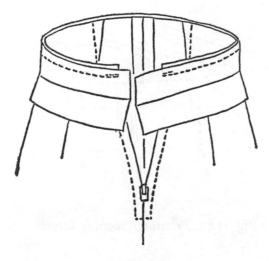

Fig. 123.   Stitching seam of waistband

Fig. 124.   Checking zipper opening to see if top is even

Trim some of the extra bulk out of the seam (Fig. 125). Trim the interfacing close to the stitching, and trim the pants side of the seam to ¼″ wide and the band seam to ⅜″. If you trim them all to the same width, you would have a thick ridge showing under the band.

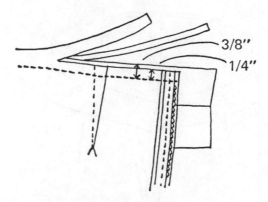

Fig. 125.   Trimming seam in layers

Press the band *up,* with the seam turned up toward the band. Press under the ⅝" seam allowance on the long edge of the band, and trim to ¼" (Fig. 126).

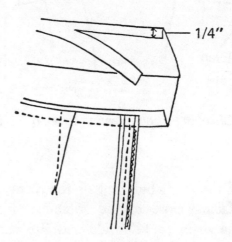

Fig. 126.   Trimming other edge of waistband

To finish the end of the band. Fold each end to the *outside* of the pants along the fold line, with the seam allowance on the long edge turned up (Fig. 127). Pin and stitch with a ⅝″ seam allowance. Trim the seams to ¼″, turn to the inside, and pin the folded edge over the waist seam. Slip-stitch by hand over the seam (Fig. 128).

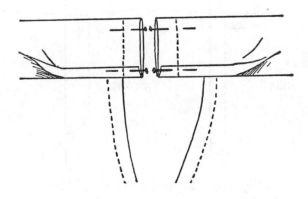

Fig. 127.   *Stitching ends of band*

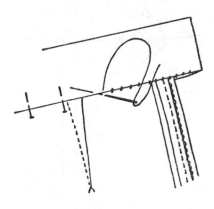

Fig. 128.   *Slip-stitching inside of band*

The waistband is made the same way for the center front or side zipper. As you look at the top of the pants with the right side out, the top edge of the band is always on your left, the underlapped edge on your right (Fig. 129).

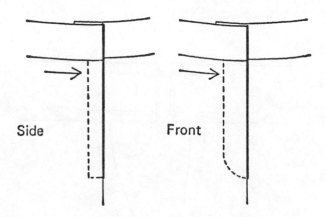

Fig. 129.   Lapped ends of waistband

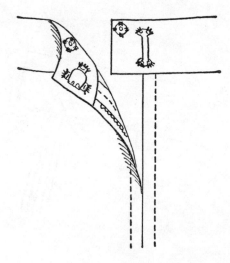

Fig. 130.   Sewing hook and eye and snap

Fasten the ends of the waistband with a hook and eye (the large flat kind is very good for pants), and a snap at the underneath corner (Fig. 130).

Hem and press the pants as described in Chapter Three.

No-waistband method. If you prefer, the same pants pattern can be made without a waistband. Grosgrain ribbon, ¾" or 1" wide, is used for an invisible inside waistband. Either the side or the center back zipper is suitable.

Measure the ribbon around your waist. It must be fitted more snugly than the regular waistband, or the pants will not stay up. Allow an extra inch, so you can turn under ½" at each end.

Mark the ribbon and the pants waist into four sections, as with the other waistband. Place the ribbon overlapping ⅝" over the top of the pants, on the right side, with ½" extending beyond each side of the zipper. Pin, and stitch close to the edge (Fig. 131).

Trim the pants seam allowance to ¼", and clip the edge at intervals of about 1", so it can be turned under smoothly (Fig. 132).

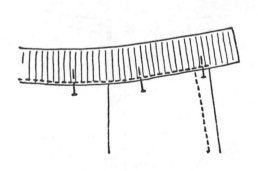

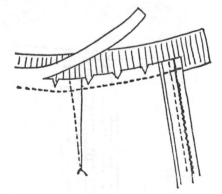

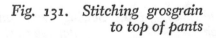

Fig. 131. *Stitching grosgrain to top of pants*

Fig. 132. *Trimming and clipping top of pants*

Turn the ribbon to the inside, and pin in place. Fold under both short ends, and slip-stitch them over the zipper tape (Fig. 133).

On the outside, topstitch ¼" from the edge (Fig. 134).

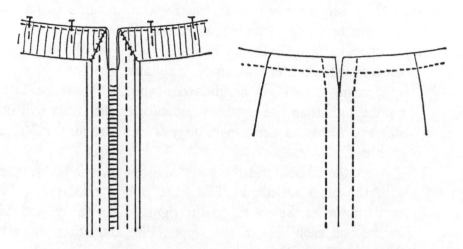

Fig. 133.   *Sewing ends of ribbon*   Fig. 134.   *Topstitching outside of waist*

For the center back zipper, fasten the top with a hook and round loop (Fig. 135). For the side-opening lapped zipper, use a hook and a flat eye (Fig. 136).

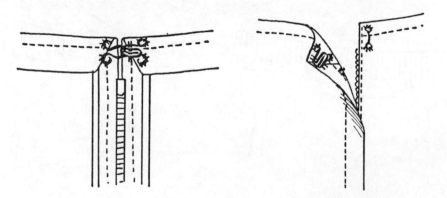

Fig. 135.   *Sewing hook and round loop to back*   Fig. 136.   *Sewing hook and flat eye to side*

Cuffs. You might like to put cuffs on some of your pants. Buy enough extra material so you can add 4″ to the length.

When finishing the bottom edge, turn up about a 4″-wide hem, then turn the cuff to the outside, making it 2″ wide (Fig. 137). You will have to experiment with this to get the length just right.

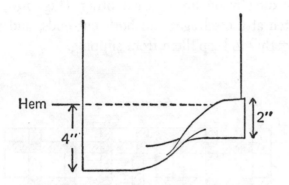

Fig. 137. Turning up a cuff

The hem edge should come just below the top of the finished cuff, and it can be machine-stitched, as it will be covered by the cuff.

Press the cuff and tack by hand at both side seams (Fig. 138).

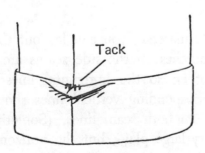

Fig. 138. Tacking cuff at seams

Matching plaids. There are special problems involved in making pants (or anything) of plaid or checked fabric. The lines of plaid must match at the center front and back, and at the two side seams. This requires extra material. For pants in a medium-size plaid, you should buy an extra ¼ yard.

Start by folding the material so that the similar lines of plaid are directly on top of each other (Fig. 139). See that they match at the selvages and both cut ends, and pin all the edges together to keep them from slipping.

Selvages

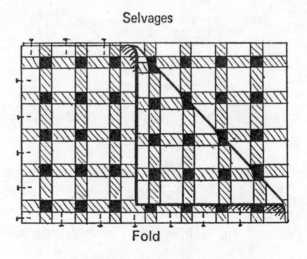

Fold

Fig. 139.   Folding plaid fabric evenly

With 60"-wide material, you can lay out the pattern as in Fig. 140. The notches on the side seams are placed directly opposite each other, so the horizontal lines will match. If possible, the corresponding vertical lines should also be the same distance from both seam lines. (Sometimes this is not possible in a very large plaid, but the horizontal matching is absolutely essential.)

Selvages

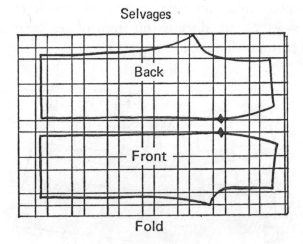

Fold

Fig. 140.   Matching plaid at side seams

With 45"-wide material, you will not be able to place the pieces opposite each other, so you must find another corresponding section of plaid (Fig. 141).

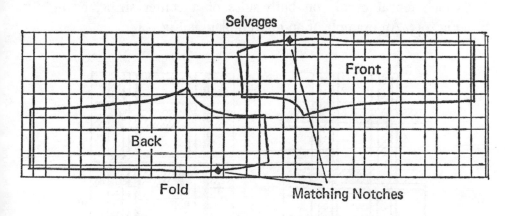

Fig. 141.   Matching plaid on 45" fabric

The center front and back seams will match because the two parts were cut directly on top of each other. The matched pattern will look like Fig. 142.

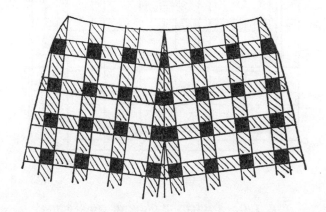

Fig. 142.   Matched plaid at center front or back

The plaid will not necessarily match on the *inside* leg seams, because the front and back are not the same shape. Plaid matching is always done in the most conspicuous seams, and the other seams must fall where they will.

The above directions apply only to *even* plaids or checks, which repeat evenly on both sides of a center stripe, as in Fig. 143. An example of an *uneven* plaid is Fig. 144.

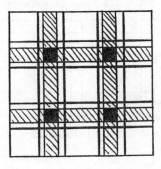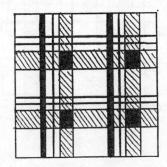

Fig. 143.   Even plaid   *Fig. 144.   Uneven plaid*

When folding this type of plaid, the blocks of the design will not come directly on top of each other. Fold it so the widest or most prominent lines come together (Fig. 145). You can match the horizontal and the prominent vertical lines, but the other vertical lines have to be ignored.

Selvages

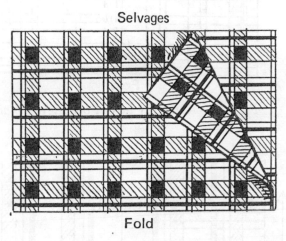

Fold

Fig. 145.   Folding uneven plaid with prominent lines together

You must be sure to use a *one-way* layout, the same as for corduroy (Fig. 146), because an uneven plaid will not be the same when turned from top to bottom. Fig. 147 shows what happens when two sections of plaid are reversed.

When stitching a seam in plaid, be sure that the lines come exactly together. Fold back the upper section along the seam line at each prominent matching line, so you can see that they meet, then pin at close intervals to prevent slipping (Fig. 148). If you always stitch the seams from *bottom* to *top*, it will help to prevent the plaid from slipping and being pushed out of alignment.

Fig. 149 shows a perfectly matched side seam.

Selvages

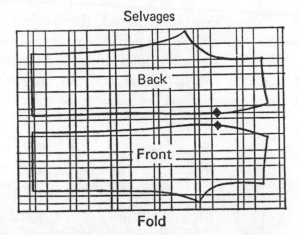

Fold

Fig. 146.   One-way layout on uneven plaid

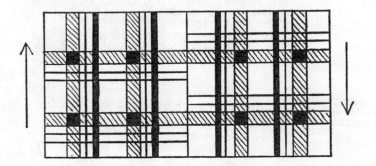

Fig. 147.   Uneven plaid running two ways

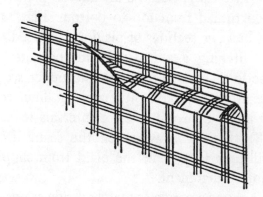

Fig. 148.   Pinning seams with plaid matched

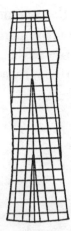

Fig. 149. Plaid matched at side seam

Lining pants. Sometimes it is desirable to put a lining in pants, especially if they are made of a scratchy wool.

Use any firmly woven lining of polyester, acetate taffeta, or various blends. Cut the lining 1″ shorter than the pants, sew it together in the same way, and leave an opening 9″ long in the seam that has the zipper.

Finish the pants all but the waistband, then put the pants and lining together with the *wrong* sides facing (Fig. 150).

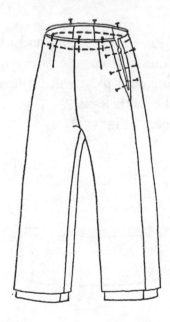

Fig. 150. Lining pinned and basted to pants

Turn under the seam allowance at the opening and pin it to the zipper tape. Pin the top edges of the pants and lining together, and machine-baste ½" from the edge.

Then attach the waistband in the usual way, and slip-stitch the lining around the zipper (Fig. 151).

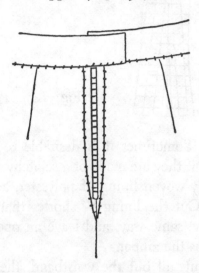

Fig. 151.   *Lining slip-stitched around zipper*

Hem the pants, then turn under ½" on the lining and pin it over the hem, about 1" from the bottom. Be sure you allow a little extra length in the lining so a pleat will form. A too-tight lining will tend to pull up the pants legs.

Slip-stitch the lining to the pants hem (Fig. 152).

Fig. 152.   *Lining slip-stitched to hem*

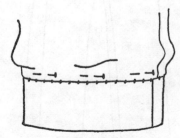

CHAPTER FIVE

Jeans (Blue, Pink, Green, or What You Will)

Blue jeans are probably the most popular and universally worn item of clothing to come along in many years. They are worn by men, women, and children, for comfort, practicality, and the casual style of dressing that so many people like.

Even if wearing jeans day in and day out is not your thing, the classic styling and fit of jeans are perfect for sportswear and can be interpreted in many different fabrics.

If you can sew basic pants, you can learn to make jeans. There are characteristics of styling and construction that distinguish jeans from other pants. They were originally intended as working clothes that would stand a lot of hard wear, so the material is very sturdy, the seams are double-stitched (in what is called a flat-felled seam) with contrasting thread, and points of extra stress are reinforced with extra stitching or nailheads.

The original classic styling has narrow legs, a fly-front closing, slanted hip pockets in front, and a pointed yoke in back with two patch pockets below it. The waistband has belt carriers and a heavy hammer-on snap at the waist (Fig. 153).

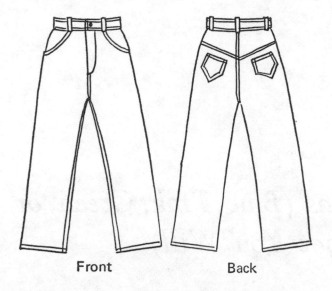

Front   Back

Fig. 153.   Classic jeans design

There are many variations in style details: bell-bottom legs, different shapes and positions of pockets, various curved yoke shapes in front or back, low-cut hip-hugger waist.

In this chapter you will learn to make the original classic jeans. You will be able to find patterns with the general style shown in Fig. 153. Sometimes a pattern will have a one-piece back yoke (Fig. 154). You can convert this to a yoke with a center back seam, which is traditional and also easier to sew.

Fig. 154.   One-piece back yoke

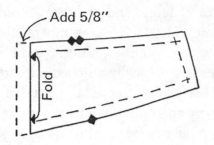

Fig. 155. Adding seam to back of yoke

The yoke pattern will look like Fig. 155, with a line to be placed on the folded material, so the pattern is cut double and opens out into the complete yoke. Add ⅝" seam allowance to the fold edge, and cut it as a two-piece yoke.

Think about using different fabrics and colors for your jeans. You can buy real blue denim, but why not try another dark or pastel denim? Try black or brown with white stitching, pastel-colored denim with dark stitching, or even a patterned material. Denim comes in plaids or checks, or a sturdy cotton with a floral print would be attractive for summer. Corduroy is fine for winter.

A smart idea for party wear is to make jeans of cotton velveteen. The contrast of casual styling with a dressy fabric has a wonderful off-beat chic, and you could make a matching velveteen jacket and a shirt of a soft silky material.

Flat-felled seams. The flat-felled seam is an essential part of any jeans, and also the topstitching on the pockets and yokes repeats the same double-stitched line. If these are not perfectly straight and even, they will look terrible, because they are done in a contrasting color and any little mistake shows up glaringly.

Before you start your jeans, practice making the flat-felled seam on scrap material until you feel confident that you can do it smoothly.

Take two pieces of fabric and pin them together along one side with the *wrong* sides facing each other. Stitch with a ⅝" seam allowance with contrasting thread, 8 to 10 stitches to the inch. *Blue* jeans are usually stitched with red, orange, or yellow thread. Heavy-duty thread is desirable and may be found where drapery and upholstery fabrics are sold.

Trim one seam allowance to ¼" (Fig. 156). Press the seam in the direction of the trimmed seam allowance, turn under ¼" on the other seam edge, and baste in place (Fig. 157). If you keep the basting a little way back from the edge of the fold, it will not get caught in the stitching.

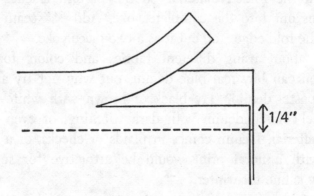

1/4"

Fig. 156.   Trimming one seam allowance

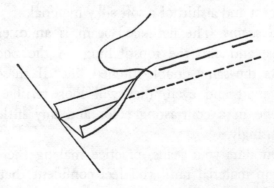

Fig. 157.   Seam edge turned under and basted

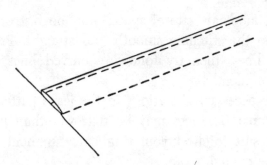

Fig. 158.   Finished flat-felled seam

Stitch close to the folded edge (Fig. 158). The two rows of stitching should be ¼" apart.

Other sections of the jeans, such as pocket edges, will be finished with two rows of topstitching, which creates a similar effect to the flat-felled seam.

To ensure that the two rows of stitches will look even, make the first row close to the outside folded edge, then line up the right edge of your presser foot so it just touches the first row of stitching. Since the distance from the needle to the edge of the presser foot (on modern machines) is ¼", the two rows of stitching will be exactly ¼" apart (Fig. 159).

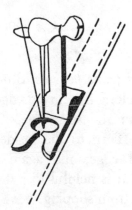

*Fig. 159.   Using presser foot
to guide stitching*

A steady, moderate rate of speed, not too fast or slow, will help to keep the stitching smooth and straight. Practice first on straight lines, then try following curved lines, until you can stitch confidently.

Make any necessary alterations in the jeans pattern, as with any other pants. The legs may be narrower than in standard pants, so be sure to check your thigh measurement to be sure you will have enough room.

Find the correct pattern layout for your size and the width of material; pin and cut all the pieces as they are shown.

The inside front pockets, shaped as in Fig. 160, are cut from a sturdy white or unbleached cotton, which can also be used for the waistband interfacing. Be sure to shrink it first.

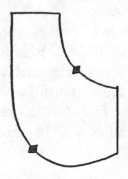

Fig. 160.   Inside front pocket

The front pockets. Stitch each pocket lining section to the front along the curved edge, right sides together (Fig. 161).

Trim the seam to ¼″, and clip the curved edges (Fig. 162). Turn to the inside, and press. Topstitch close to the folded edge, and again ¼″ from the first stitching (Fig. 163). It is helpful to put pins along the edge to keep the two layers from slipping.

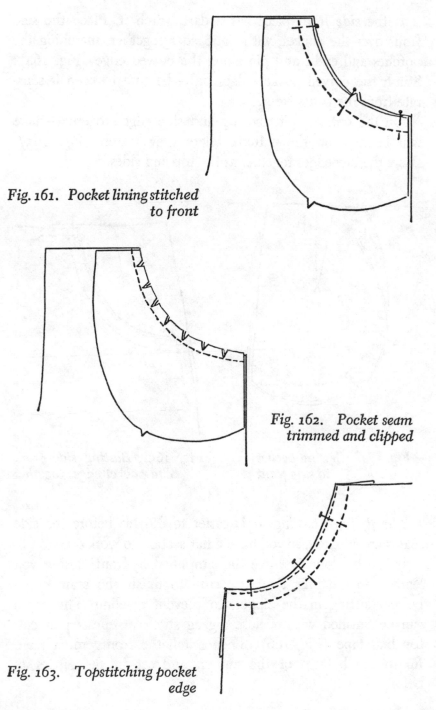

Fig. 161. *Pocket lining stitched to front*

Fig. 162. *Pocket seam trimmed and clipped*

Fig. 163. *Topstitching pocket edge*

If the *side front* piece has a dart, stitch it. Place the side front over the pocket, with right sides together, matching the notches and ends, and pin along the curved edge (Fig. 164). Stitch the curved pocket edges only—be sure to keep it separate from the pants front.

On the outside, pin the top and side edges together—there will be dots on the pattern where they match (Fig. 165). Baste the raw edges together at the top and sides.

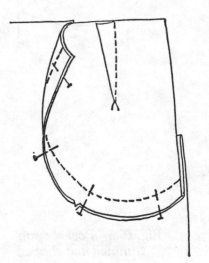

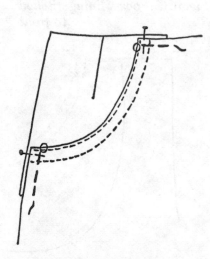

Fig. 164. *Sewing pocket to side front*   Fig. 165. *Basting side front and pocket edges together*

The fly-front closing. It is easier to do this before the side seams are stitched, so you have a flat section to work on.

It can be done just like the simplified fly-front closing you learned in Chapter Four. Be sure to finish the seam edges before putting in the zipper, to prevent raveling. The edges can be finished with a close zigzag stitch or encased in cotton bias tape (Fig. 166). Then stitch the front crotch seam up to the bottom of the zipper, and set in the zipper as before.

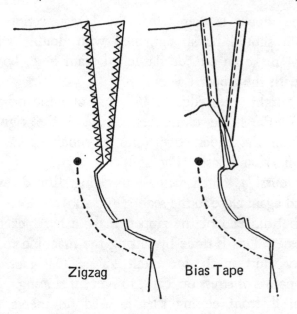

Zigzag   Bias Tape

Fig. 166.   Finishing seam edges

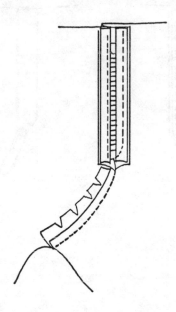

Fig. 167.   Trimming and clipping crotch seam

After the zipper is completed, the lower section of the crotch seam should be strengthened with double stitching. You cannot make an *outside* flat-felled seam here, because it interferes with the zipper.

Trim the right seam edge to ¼", and clip the other seam (Fig. 167). Press the entire seam toward the right, turn under ¼" on the wider edge (clip as much as needed to make it lie flat), and baste (Fig. 168).

On the *outside*, stitch with contrasting thread over the basting, and again close to the seam (Fig. 169).

At the bottom end of the zipper, make a bar tack through all thicknesses. This is done by setting the machine to zigzag, with a very short stitch, for about ½". A bar tack can be used at all points of stress on jeans, to prevent ripping.

The real fly-front closing that is used on men's trousers and all commercially made jeans is somewhat more compli-

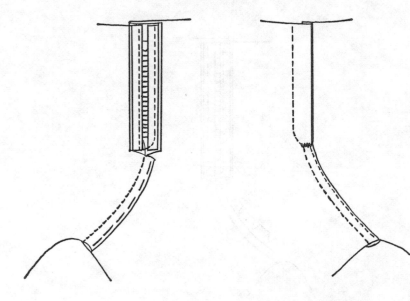

Fig. 168. *Seam edge turned under and basted*   Fig. 169. *Stitching seam on outside*

cated, but it can be mastered if you would like your jeans to be the genuine article.

It is traditional on men's clothes for all zipper or buttoned closings to open toward the *right*. Girls' jeans are also made this way, for the real man-tailored look.

If your pattern does not provide for this type of fly opening, you will have to make a few additions to it. If the front has an extra extension beyond the seam, cut it off. Mark a stitching line 1⅛″ from the seam line, parallel to the edge, and a horizontal line ¼″ below the dot marking the bottom of the zipper (Fig. 170). Round off the corner where the two lines cross.

You need a pattern for the fly facing. Pin a piece of tissue paper over the front pants pattern (Fig. 171). Trace the curved stitching line and the front and top edges. Add ⅝″

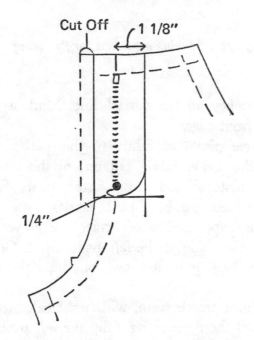

Fig. 170.   *Marking fly front on pattern*

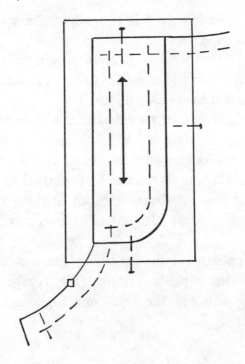

Fig. 171.   Making a pattern for fly facing

seam allowance beyond the curved line. Mark a grain line parallel to the front edge.

Cut out three pieces of fabric to this pattern. If using corduroy or other heavy fabric, cut one of the pieces of the pocket lining material and two of the pants fabric. For denim, all three pieces can be of pants fabric.

With tracing paper and wheel, trace the curved stitching line onto the *wrong* side of the *left* pants front. Go over the line with hand basting so it shows on the right side (Fig. 172).

Stitch the front crotch seam, with right sides together, as far as the end of the fly marking. Clip the *left* pants seam allowance at the top of the seam (Fig. 173).

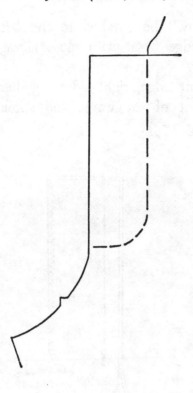

Fig. 172.   *Marking stitching line*

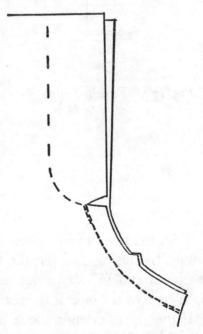

Fig. 173.   *Stitching and clipping crotch seam*

One piece of the fly facing will be stitched to the *left* front. Clean-finish the curved edge of it with close zigzag stitching (Fig. 174).

Pin the facing to the *left* front edge, right sides together (folding the right side down out of the way), and stitch from the top as far as the clip (Fig. 175).

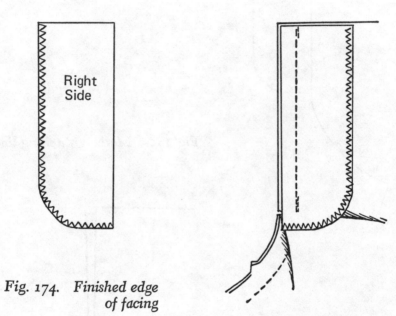

Fig. 174.   *Finished edge of facing*

Fig. 175.   *Stitching facing to left edge*

Trim the seam to ¼", press the facing out, with the seams toward the facing, and pin the closed zipper, *face down*, with the lower end ¼" above the end of the fly marking, and the right edge of the tape at the seam (Fig. 176).

If the zipper extends above the upper edge, it doesn't matter. This will be cut off later.

Stitch close to the *left* edge of the tape, and again ¼″ to the right of the first stitching, using a zipper foot.

Press the fly facing and zipper to the inside along the seam, and baste through all thicknesses along the curved edge (Fig. 177). Pin the end of the right zipper tape out of the way.

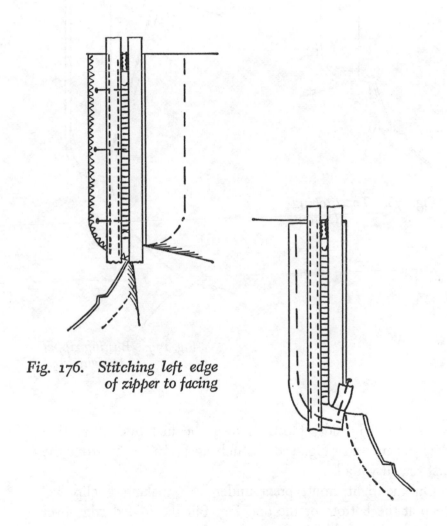

Fig. 176. *Stitching left edge*
of zipper to facing

Fig. 177. *Basting edge of fly facing*

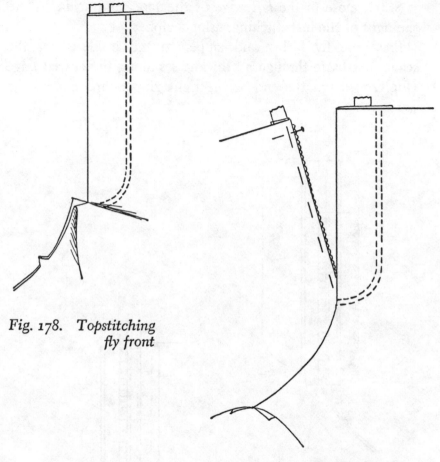

Fig. 178.   *Topstitching fly front*

Fig. 179.   *Basting zipper to right front*

On the right side, topstitch over the first line of basting that you marked (Fig. 178). Stitch again ⅛" away from the first row, if you like.

On the right front, press under ⅜", making a clip ⅜" deep at the bottom of the opening. Pin the folded edge over the *open* zipper, close to the teeth, and baste (Fig. 179).

You will have an overlap of ¼" when the zipper is closed.

Now you will make a shield that goes underneath the right side of the zipper. Use the other facing piece and the piece cut from lining fabric, and pin them with right sides together. Stitch ⅝" from the curved edge (Fig. 180). Trim the seam to ¼", turn, and press.

To finish the open edge, trim ⅜" from the pants fabric, turn the lining over it, pin, and stitch close to the edge (Fig. 181).

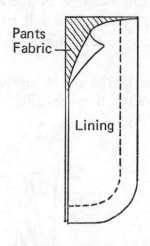

Fig. 180. *Stitching lining to fly shield*

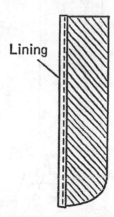

Fig. 181. *Finishing open edge of shield*

Working on the inside, place the shield under the right front, with the pants fabric side facing the closed zipper. Match the top edges and match the curved edge to the line of topstitching, and pin in place (Fig. 182).

On the *outside*, pin the right front and zipper to the shield (Fig. 183). Open the zipper and remove the pins that you placed in the wrong side. Stitch close to the fold through all thicknesses, holding the left side out of the way (Fig. 184).

With the zipper *open*, stitch across the tops of the zipper tapes, and cut off the extra zipper. These ends will later be sewn into the waistband so the zipper tab cannot slide off (Fig. 185).

Finish the lower crotch seam as in the directions for the simplified fly front, pressing it toward the *left* (Fig. 186). Make a bar tack at the bottom of the zipper.

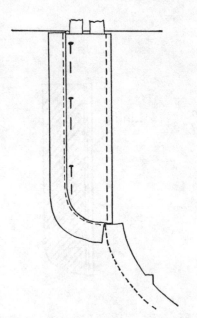

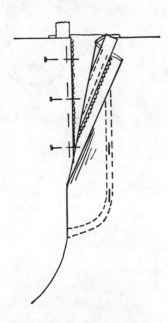

Fig. 182.   *Shield pinned in place*   Fig. 183.   *Right front and zipper pinned to shield*

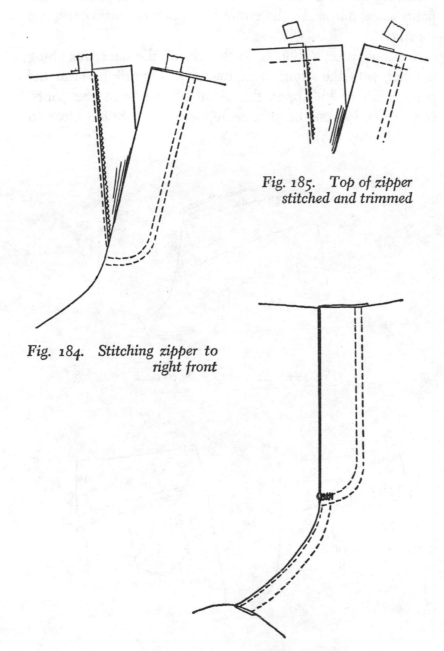

Fig. 185. *Top of zipper stitched and trimmed*

Fig. 184. *Stitching zipper to right front*

Fig. 186. *Topstitching crotch seam*

Sewing the pants back. Now you can put the front of the pants aside, and make the entire back, before putting the two together.

Sew one yoke section to each side of the back, matching notches, with the *wrong* sides together (Fig. 187). Trim the pants seam to ¼", press the seam down toward the pants, turn under ¼" on the yoke seam, and baste. Stitch close to the fold (Fig. 188).

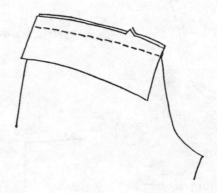

Fig. 187.   *Stitching yoke to back*

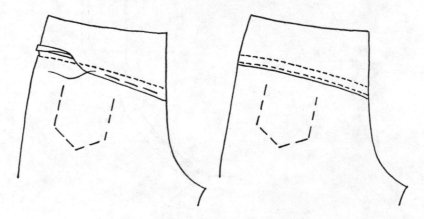

Fig. 188.   *Topstitching yoke*

The back pockets will be made now. It is easier to do them while you have two flat sections to work on.

Mark the position of the pockets on the wrong side with tracing paper, and transfer the markings to the outside with basting thread or pins. (Be sure to remove the pins before stitching.)

Turn under ⅝" on the top edge of the pocket, fold under the raw edge ¼", and stitch close to the fold and again along the edge (Fig. 189).

Jeans often have decorative stitching on the back pockets, and if you want to try this, it is done before attaching the pocket. Double rows of stitching can make initials or a simple geometric design. Examples are shown in Fig. 190.

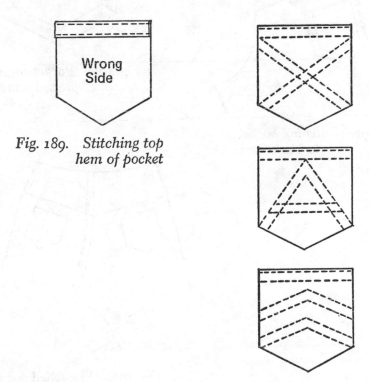

Fig. 189.   *Stitching top hem of pocket*

Fig. 190.   *Designs for back pocket*

First draw your design with tailor's chalk and a ruler. After the design is stitched, the chalk can be brushed off.

Press under ⅝" on the remaining pocket edges (Fig. 191).

Place the pocket over the marked position lines, pin, and stitch close to the edge. Stitch again ¼" from the edge (Fig. 192).

Stitch the entire back crotch seam. Finish with a flat-felled seam turned toward the right (Fig. 193).

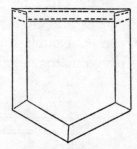

Fig. 191.   Pocket edges pressed under

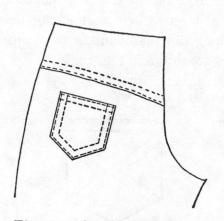

Fig. 192.   Stitching pocket to pants back

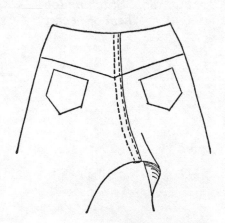

Fig. 193.   Flat-felled seam on back crotch

Stitching the side and inside leg seams. You must decide which set of seams will have the flat-felled seams. This must be done while the pants are opened out flat, because it would be next to impossible to do the outside topstitching after the pants legs are stitched up.

Let us say you decide to have the flat-felled seams at the sides. Stitch both side seams with the wrong sides together, and trim the back seam allowances to ¼" (Fig. 194).

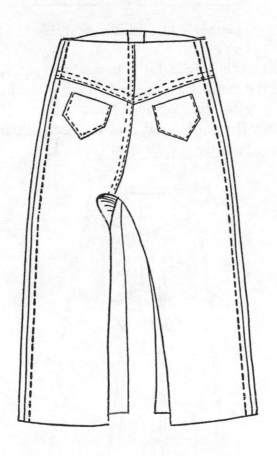

Fig. 194. Stitching side seams

Spread the pants legs out flat, fold the front seam allowance over the back, and topstitch (Fig. 195).

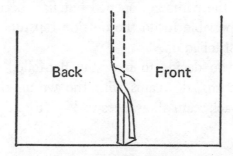

Back   Front

Fig. 195.   Flat-felled seam at sides

Stitch the entire inside leg seams in one piece, matching the ends of the crotch seams, with *right* sides together.

Make a row of close zigzag stitching about ¼″ from the first stitching (Fig. 196), and trim the seam allowances close to the zigzag. Press the seam toward the back.

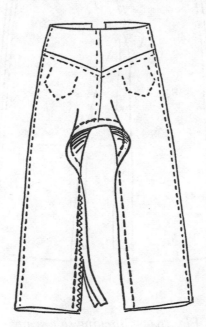

Fig. 196.   Zigzag finish on inside leg seams

This makes a good strong seam, although there is no decorative outside stitching.

If you prefer to have the inner leg seams done with a flat-felled seam, do that first, then finish the side seams with zig-zag on the inside, and press toward the back.

Waistband. Your pattern may specify either a curved or a straight waistband. A curved waistband allows the pants to fit lower at the waist. Make whichever your pattern calls for.

The straight waistband can be made exactly as in Chapter Four, or you can use a shortcut that eliminates all hand sewing. Jeans, after all, should look sturdy and machine-made.

Sew the *right* side of the waistband (the part without interfacing) to the *wrong* side of the pants (Fig. 197). Finish the ends even with both edges of the fly opening. Turn to the outside, turn under the long edges, pin, and topstitch close to the fold. Topstitch also the top edge and two front ends (Fig. 198).

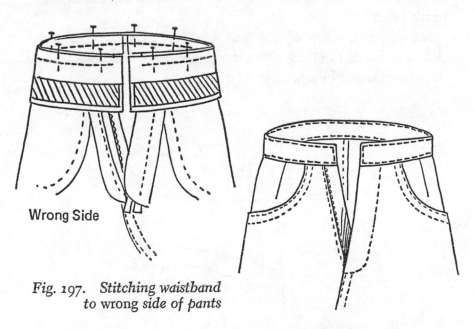

Wrong Side

Fig. 197. Stitching waistband to wrong *side of pants*

Fig. 198. Topstitched waistband

The curved waistband has one back section and two front sections, with side seams. Baste interfacing to each section, or use fusible interfacing. Stitch the two side seams and press open (Fig. 199).

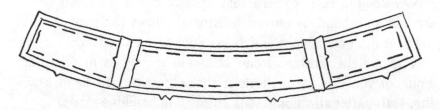

Fig. 199.   Stitching seams of curved waistband

Pin the band to the top of the pants and check the fit. The ends extend ⅝″ beyond the fly opening. (If using the *simplified* fly front, allow at least 1″ of overlap on the underneath side.)

Stay-stitch the top of the pants ½″ from the edge, and clip at intervals of about 1″ so the pants top will spread to fit the curved edge of the waistband (Fig. 200).

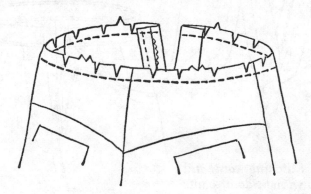

Fig. 200.   Stay-stitching and clipping top of pants

Pin the lower edge of the waistband to the top of the pants, right sides togeher, matching side seams, notches, and center back (Fig. 201). Front edges extend ⅝" beyond fly edges.

Stitch, trim seam to ¼", and press band and seam up (Fig. 202).

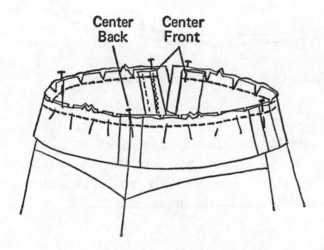

Fig. 201.   Stitching waistband to pants

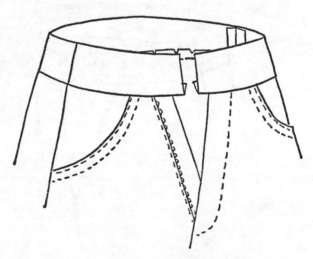

Fig. 202.   Waistband and seam pressed up

Stitch the waistband facing pieces at the sides. Press up
⅝″ on the bottom edge and trim to ¼″ (Fig. 203).

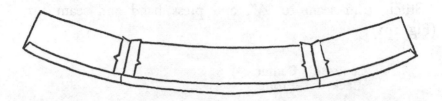

Fig. 203. Waistband facing with edge pressed up

Pin the facing over the waistband, right sides together,
matching seams, ends, and center back, and stitch top and
both ends with a ⅝″ seam allowance (Fig. 204). Trim the
seams, to ¼″, and corners and clip the upper edge.

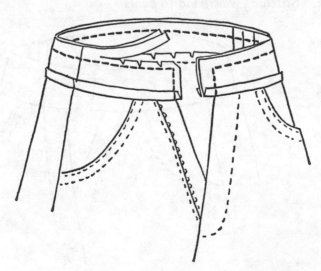

Fig. 204. Stitching facing to waistband

Turn the facing to the inside and press. Pin the folded edge over the seam and slip-stitch (Fig. 205).

On the outside, topstitch the waistband close to both edges and the ends (Fig. 206).

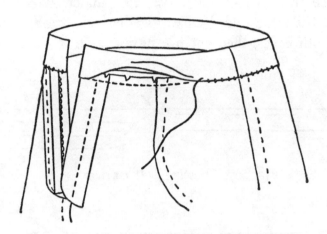

Fig. 205. Slip-stitching facing over the seam

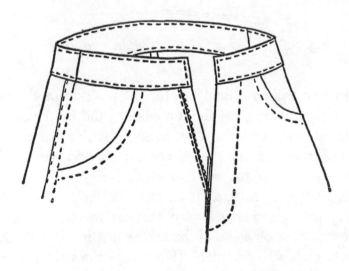

Fig. 206. Topstitched waistband

Belt Carriers. To make five belt carriers, it is easiest to cut and sew one long strip, then cut it into five pieces.

Cut a straight strip of fabric 1⅜" wide by 20" long. (If you do not have any long pieces of leftovers, make several short lengths.)

Fold the strip in half lengthwise, fold under ¼" on each edge, and baste the folded edges together (Fig. 207). Stitch close to both edges, then cut five pieces, each 4" long (Fig. 208).

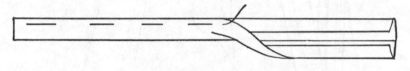

Fig. 207. Basting belt carriers

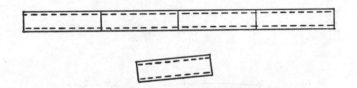

Fig. 208. Stitching and cutting belt carriers

The pattern will have markings for the position of the belt carriers. They usually go at the top edge of the front pockets, at the center back, and about 1" in back of the side seams.

Fold under ½" on one end of the carrier, and pin it even with the top edge of the waistband (Fig. 209). Turn under the other end and pin it so it extends ½" below the waistband. Try the belt that you plan to wear to see if there is room enough. Cut off some of the carrier if it is too long. Sew across both ends with a bar tack (Fig. 210)—the same way you finished the bottom of the zipper.

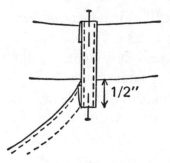

Fig. 209. *Pinning belt carriers*

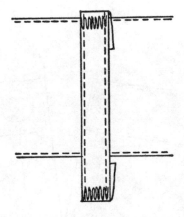

Fig. 210. *Sewing belt carriers
with bar tack*

Finishing. Try on the jeans and adjust the length. Cut off all but ⅝" hem allowance, and turn under ¼" on the edge. Turn hem to inside of pants leg, and stitch close to the edge of the hem (Fig. 211).

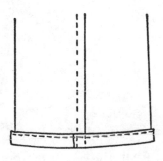

Fig. 211 *Stitched hem*

The waistband can be finished with a hammer-on snap (Fig. 212). You can buy kits with the necessary tools and instructions. Be sure to get the extra-heavy-duty type, as the smaller ones will not go through the heavy fabric.

If you prefer, you can make a machine buttonhole in the left side, and there are special metal buttons that are made especially for jeans (Fig. 213).

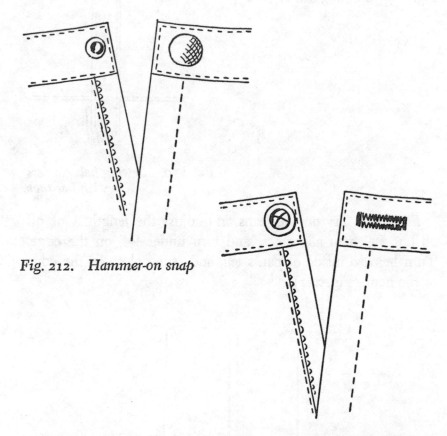

Fig. 212.   *Hammer-on snap*

Fig. 213.   *Button and buttonhole*

The top corners of all the pockets should be reinforced. Use bar tacks (Fig. 214).

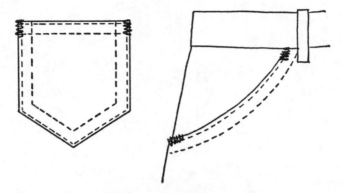

Fig. 214.   Bar tacks on pockets

Nailheads, available in most fabric stores, can be used instead. They look authentic and are very strong (Fig. 215). There are two prongs, which are pushed through to the wrong side of the material. It may help to start the holes with the point of your scissors.

On the wrong side, bend the two prongs toward each other, using a thimble, then finish by flattening with a hammer.

To prevent the prongs from scratching or tearing your clothes, sew a small piece of cotton seam tape over the wrong side of the nailhead (Fig. 216).

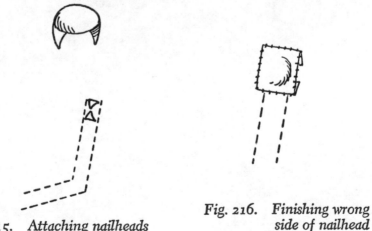

Fig. 216.   Finishing wrong side of nailhead

Fig. 215.   Attaching nailheads

CHAPTER SIX

Pants in Variety

Besides the basic long pants and jeans, many other styles and lengths of pants are popular. The construction method is the same for all. Different kinds of pockets or shaped yokes are variations on what you have already learned.

For warm weather you will probably want shorts. The very short length is good for tennis or other active sports; then there is a medium length, usually called Jamaica, and the Bermuda length, which stops just above the knee (Fig. 217). Any of them may have cuffs.

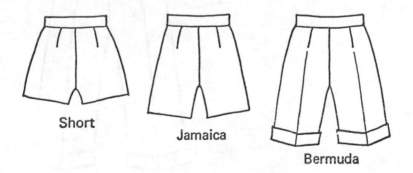

Short   Jamaica   Bermuda

Fig. 217.   3 styles of shorts

Culottes, or gaucho pants, are cut full, like a skirt, and come to a little below the knee or to mid-calf (Fig. 218). When made of tweed or flannel, this style looks especially smart worn with high boots.

Fig. 218.   Gaucho pants

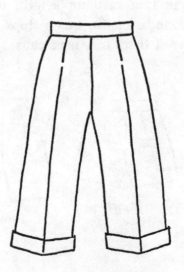

Fig. 219.   Clam-diggers

Standard straight-legged pants that stop somewhere below the knee are called clam-diggers (Fig. 219).

Knickers are a style that stages a comeback every few years (Fig. 220). They are not the most becoming style for everyone, but a slim, well-proportioned girl with a good sense of style can get away with them. When worn with boots or patterned knee socks, with a tailored shirt or bulky sweater on top, they create an appealing little-boy look.

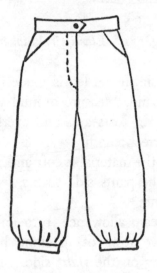

Fig. 220.   Knickers

Knickers. You can make knickers from a regular pants pattern with a straight leg. Allow enough length so they will blouse slightly below the knee, and add an extra inch if using an elastic casing or a ⅝″ seam allowance if you are going to attach a fabric band.

The elastic casing is made just the same as the top of the pants in Chapter Three. Use ¾"-wide elastic, and fit it just tightly enough to hold the pants in place (Fig. 221).

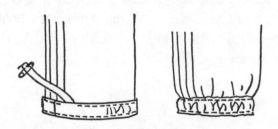

Fig. 221.   Elastic in knickers

A fabric band to finish the leg is made in the same way as a plain pants waistband. Measure around your leg just below the knee, and add 2½" for seams and overlap. Cut two strips 3¼" wide by the correct length.

Use interfacing if the material is soft and stretchy.

When stitching the pants side seams, leave an opening 3" long at each lower end.

Press under the seam allowance, turn under the raw edges, and hem. Stitch two rows of machine basting around the bottom edge, working on the *right* side. The first row should be ⅝" from the edge, the second row ¼" closer to the edge (Fig. 222).

Fold the band in half lengthwise, right side out, and press. Also press up ⅝" on one long edge. On the other edge, mark the correct finished length of the band with one pin ⅝" from the right edge, and measure from the first pin the exact length and mark with another pin (Fig. 223). The extra length is the back underlap.

This is the band for the left leg. The right-leg band is marked with the pins in the opposite position.

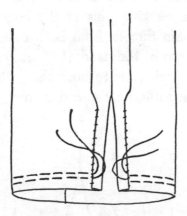

Fig. 222.   *Gathering leg edge of knickers*

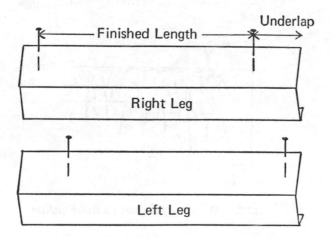

Fig. 223.   *Measuring leg band of knickers*

Pin the band to the bottom of the pant leg, right sides together, with the marking pins at the edges of the opening.
Pull up the bobbin threads from both ends until the edge is
gathered enough to fit the band (Fig. 224). Wind the thread
around a pin at both ends to hold the gathers in place (Fig.
225). Be sure the gathers are spread evenly.

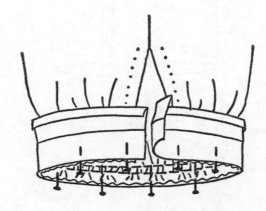

Fig. 224.   Pinning leg band to gathered edge

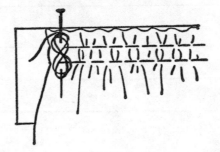

Fig. 225.   Winding thread to hold gathers

Stitch on the side with the gathers, then trim the seam to
¼", stitch the two short ends, and turn the band to the inside. Hem the folded edge over the seam (Fig. 226).

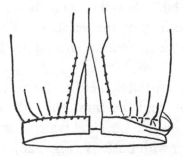

Fig. 226.   Finishing inside of leg band

This is exactly the same method as the one for the pants waistband in Chapter Four. The only difference is the gathers. This is also the way you would attach a waistband to a gathered skirt.

On the outside, lap the front edge of the band over the back, with the extension underneath. Let the opening edges just meet, and fasten the band with a hook and eye (Fig. 227).

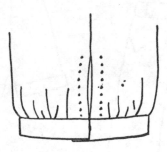

Fig. 227.   Leg band lapped front to back

Overalls and jump suits. Overalls, either long or short, are very popular with young girls, and the jump suit (an all-in-one garment of pants and top) is an attractive and comfortable style for almost anyone.

Overalls have a bib front that may be cut in one piece with the pants or seamed at the waist. Usually the entire bib front is a double layer of fabric. The zipper is in the center back.

Straps are made separately, either sewn on at the back waist or buttoned on, and the front ends of the straps can be fastened with real overall buckles, which can be bought in many fabric stores, or with buttons (Fig. 228).

The only different fitting problem is to get the length of the straps just right. Before the straps are sewn in place, try the overalls on and have a friend pin the straps in the back. If you are short-waisted they will need to be shortened.

Individual patterns will give you directions for making the particular style of overall you have chosen.

Fig. 228. Long or short overalls

Jump suits can be as casual as mechanics' coveralls, or dressy halter-necked evening pajamas. There is a special problem in fitting jump suits, because the upper part must be adjusted to fit your waist length. Since it is attached to the pants, it will affect the crotch depth. If the upper part is too long, you will have a droopy fit in the crotch, and if it is too short, you will not have room to sit down.

The front and back pattern pieces of a jump suit will look something like Fig. 229. There are horizontal lines across the waist, indicating where to lengthen or shorten it.

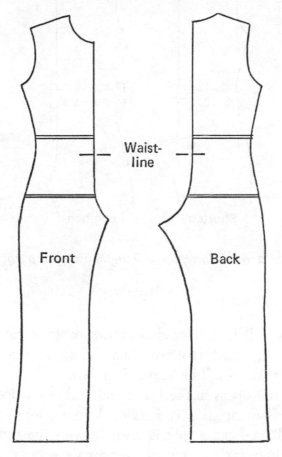

Waist-line

Front

Back

Fig. 229.   Typical jump suit pattern

Have someone measure your back waist length, then compare it with the corresponding measurement on your pattern envelope.

Adjust both the front and back of the pattern as necessary (Fig. 230), using the same method as in Chapter Two, Figs. 14 and 15.

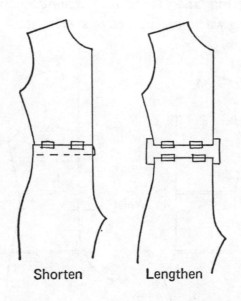

Shorten   Lengthen

Fig. 230.   Shortening or lengthening jump suit

Make any alterations needed in the pants section, as you would for any pants pattern. Some designs have a loose-fitting waist, which will be held in by a belt.

A jump suit opens in the front, with either a zipper or buttons. The front opening is finished before joining the front to the back, and the zipper is sewn in with the centered application (Fig. 231), or an invisible zipper may be used.

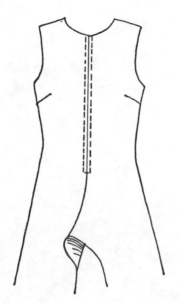

Fig. 231.   Front zipper in jump suit

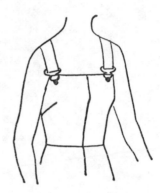

Fig. 232.   Overall cut high at top

The sleeves, collar, pockets, and so on, of a jump suit can be in a great variety of styles. If you are not an experienced sewer, you can find patterns labeled "Simple" or "Beginners" with directions that will be easy to follow for one who has already learned to make pants.

There is an overall style that is cut high enough at the top to be worn without a blouse (Fig. 232). The zipper is in the back. This should be considered in the same class as a jump suit in regard to fitting. The length of the front and back waist should be lengthened or shortened as necessary, and the length of the straps also usually needs some adjustment.

CHAPTER SEVEN

Alterations and Remodeling

If you do not have a perfect model's figure, you know that it is hard to buy ready-made pants to fit exactly right.

If you are very short or tall, try to buy proportioned-length pants. Not only will they fit better in the length of the leg, but the length of the crotch will also be in better proportion for a short or tall woman.

If you still can't get the exact fit in proportioned pants, there are several fairly simple alterations that you can make.

Altering the length. The length is the easiest thing to change. If pants are too long, take out the old hem, and cut off some of the extra length (a 2" or 3" hem is enough).

The raw edge of the hem must be finished, either with a row of zigzag stitching or with seam binding; then follow the directions for sewing a hem in Chapter Three.

Pants can be lengthened if there is a fairly generous hem. Be sure to check on this before buying.

Take out the hem, and press with a damp cloth to remove the crease. A facing should be sewn to the bottom edge, so you will have some width to turn up. Pants do not hang properly with a very narrow hem.

You can buy 2"-wide bias hem facing in many colors, or

use scraps of lining fabric. (For pants, this can be cut either straight or bias.)

Fold out one of the turned edges of the bias hem facing, pin to the bottom of the pants, right sides together, matching the edges, and lap the ends, with one end turned under for a neat finish (Fig. 233). Pin, and stitch in the groove of the fold.

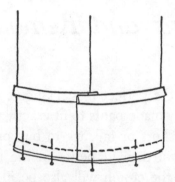

Fig. 233.   Stitching facing to bottom of pants

Turn to the inside, with the facing seam slightly above the bottom edge so it will not show on the outside, and hem as usual (Fig. 234). Also hem the lapped end of the facing.

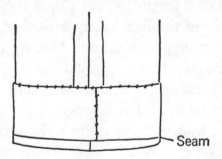

Fig. 234.   Hemming pants with facing

Altering the waist size. Pants that are large enough to fit wide hips may be too loose in the waist, so the waist must be taken in. Never plan to buy a smaller waist size and let out the hips, as there is usually not enough seam allowance for that.

With elastic-waist pants, all you need to do is shorten the elastic. Rip out a few inches of the elastic casing, pull out the elastic, cut, and lap one end over the other and pin (Fig. 235). Try on and adjust the size. Stitch the ends of the elastic firmly together, slide it back into the casing, and sew up the opening.

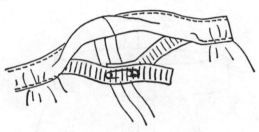

Fig. 235. *Shortening waist elastic*

Some pants have an attached waistband with the elastic sewn into the seam. Rip out a few inches of waistband at both side seams (or at the center back) and open it out flat. Stitch in as much as needed, going right through the elastic and waistband, and taper gradually to a few inches below the waist (Fig. 236). Trim off the excess material, press the seam, turn the waistband down, and sew over the elastic.

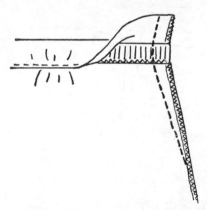

Fig. 236. *Taking in side of pants with elastic*

For pants with a regular waistband: sometimes in jeans or real man-tailored pants there is a back seam that goes right up through the waistband (Fig. 237). It is quite simple to stitch this in as much as needed, tapering it gradually to a few inches below the waist (Fig. 238). Rip out the old seam, trim off some of the excess, and press the seam open.

Center Back

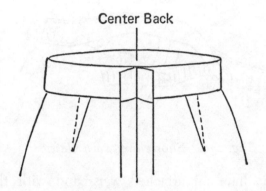

Fig. 237.   Back seam through waistband

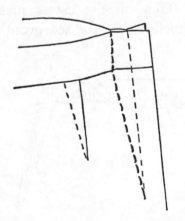

Fig. 238.   Taking in back seam

If the waistband does not have a seam in the back, the job is a little more complicated. You could take off the waistband all the way back to one end of the zipper, but to avoid that, you can do it this way:

Take out the waistband stitching for a few inches across the back. Take in the back seam, and also the darts can be taken in a little. Take in a corresponding amount at the center of the waistband (Fig. 239). Trim and press the seam open, then sew the waistband in place again.

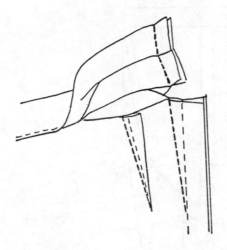

Fig. 239. Taking in back seam with separate waistband

Altering the crotch depth. You have learned that the crotch depth is one of the most important fitting points. If the crotch is too short and tight in ready-made pants, there is not much you can do. It is best to buy a larger size and take it in at the waist and hips.

However, there is a way of adding a little extra crotch depth that will work if you are tall but not too heavy in the hips.

Turn the pants wrong side out, with one leg slipped down inside the other. Notice the shape of the crotch seam (Fig. 240). You can see that if you take in a deeper seam at the bottom of the curve, you will actually be adding more length.

You can get as much as an extra ½″ of length here. Do not try to stitch the seam any deeper than that, because you will be too far down into the narrower part of the leg. Double-stitch or zigzag-stitch the seam, and trim it off close (Fig. 241).

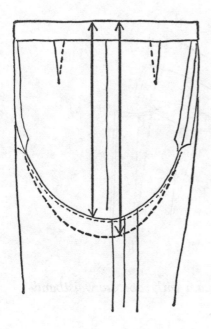

Fig. 240. Adding length to crotch of pants

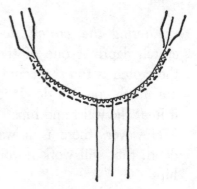

Fig. 241. Crotch seam trimmed and finished with zigzag

If the crotch depth is too long all around, you will have to remove the entire waistband, cut off as much as necessary at the top, and replace the waistband.

Usually, though, the problem is with extra fullness only in the back of the pants. Have a friend pin up a tuck across the back of the pants until it fits smoothly, tapering to nothing at the side seams (Fig. 242).

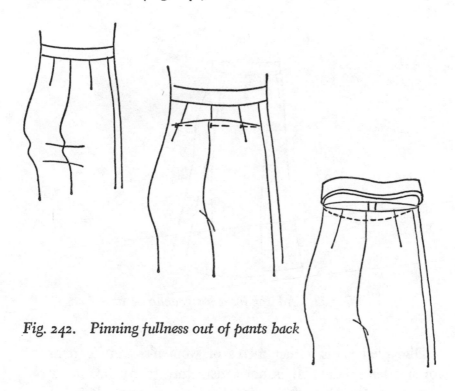

Fig. 242. Pinning fullness out of pants back

Fig. 243. Marking new waistline in back

Remove the back waistband between the side seams. Measure down from the top how much you need to take off at the center back, and draw a chalk line, tapering to nothing at both side seams (Fig. 243). Cut off along the line, and replace the waistband.

Remodeling old pants. If you have old favorite pants that are now too short, consider cutting them off for shorts, clam-diggers, or knickers (see Chapter Six). The extra cut-off fabric can be used to make bands for the knickers.

You might make gaucho pants by making the legs wider. Rip out both side seams to within a few inches of the top, and set in a long triangle of fabric taken from the cut-off legs (Fig. 244).

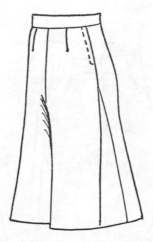

Fig. 244.   Adding inset for gaucho pants

Discarded pants, either men's or women's, can be remade for smaller children. It is not satisfactory to try taking in or shortening the pants if the size difference is great. It is better to start from scratch: rip out all the seams, press, and cut out from a child's pattern.

Children grow so fast that pants may suddenly be discovered to be halfway up the leg. Contrasting trim can be added for length, and looks cute for kids, though it might look rather tacky for adult clothes. Blue jeans are especially good for this treatment.

Try a contrasting turned-up cuff, with knee patches to match (Fig. 245).

Fig. 245.   Adding cuffs and knee patches to jeans

Wide braid added to the bottom can be repeated for trim on the side seams (Fig. 246). Use two rows on the bottom if necessary.

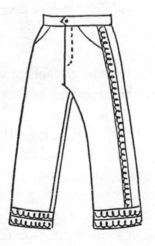

Fig. 246.   Adding braid trim

Kids and teens like to wear jeans that look tattered and patched, so you can have fun adding all kinds of appliqué trim and patches.

Rickrack braid can be stitched over frayed seams to add longer life and colorful trim as well. Add extra rows for more decorative effect (Fig. 247).

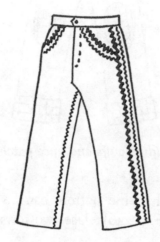

Fig. 247. *Adding rickrack over seams*

Bands added to the bottom can be of any irregular shape, and the material can be repeated in appliqué motifs (Fig. 248).

When applying odd-shaped patches, attach them first with an iron-on bonding material (available in several different brands in fabric shops), then stitch around the raw edges with a row of very close zigzag stitching (Fig. 249).

If your sewing machine does embroidery stitches, experiment with it by dreaming up some embroidered trimming for your jeans.

Fig. 248.   Decorative bands and appliqués

Fig. 249.   Appliqué attached with zigzag

CHAPTER EIGHT

Building a Pants Wardrobe

With a few well-tailored pairs of pants, co-ordinating tops, and an assortment of accessories, you can be well dressed for almost any occasion.

Here are suggestions for a minimum basic wardrobe. Extras can be added according to your taste and the amount of money you can spend.

Choose a basic color that you really like. If the important items are in shades of brown, black, navy, beige, or gray, everything will fit together, and you can add other items in bright colors that will go with them.

Start with a matching blazer and pants (Fig. 250), and add a second pair of pants in a co-ordinated plaid or check. (Or you could begin, instead, with a plaid jacket and pants, and add plain dark pants.)

A third pair of pants can be in a lighter or brighter color, perhaps picking up one of the colors of the plaid.

A sleeveless vest can repeat one of the other fabrics; or choose a bright contrasting color (Fig. 251).

Fig. 250.   *Matching blazer
and pants*

Fig. 251.   *Co-ordinated plaid
pants, contrasting vest*

Have several lightweight tailored shirts: one white, one solid-color, and one patterned (Fig. 252).

You will need at least two or three pullover sweaters or turtleneck jerseys, in assorted colors (Fig. 253).

Fig. 253.   Extra pants with assorted sweaters

Fig. 252.   Tailored shirts

Your faithful blue jeans are combined with T-shirts in assorted plain colors or stripes, which can also be worn with the other pants (Fig. 254).

For dressy occasions, use a soft, silky material for a bow-tied or ruffled blouse to wear with the dark pants, or try a

pair of velveteen jeans. If you like, add a velveteen jacket
(Fig. 255), either a blazer or a shorter western style, in a
color that can be worn with your other pants for more casual
occasions. Velveteen has the wonderful quality of looking
right at any time of the day or night.

Fig. 255.   Dressy blouse, pants, and jacket

Accessories. Chunky, medium-heeled shoes, cut high in front (Fig. 256) look right with most pants. Boots (Fig. 257) are a must, and not just for stormy weather. Wear them with your jeans tucked in, or underneath wider pants; and they look great with gaucho pants or knickers, as well as skirts.

Have at least one pair of comfortable, flat, knockabout shoes (Fig. 258) to wear with jeans for active outdoor occasions.

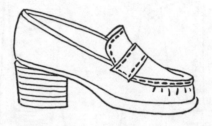

Fig. 256.   Chunky shoes for pants

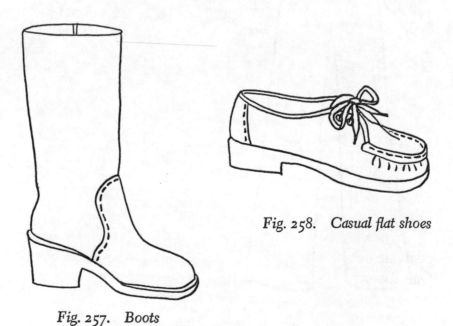

Fig. 258.   Casual flat shoes

Fig. 257.   Boots

Fig. 259.   Dressy sandals

Fig. 260.   Dressy and casual handbags

One dressy pair of shoes, with a higher but chunky heel (Fig. 259) will go with evening pants as well as with dresses. Sandals are now worn year round and look fine with pants.

One roomy shoulder bag in your basic color can be used every day, and a small, neat bag is needed to carry with dressy outfits (Fig. 260).

For winter, wear a cozy knitted hat, a long muffler, and wool or lined leather gloves (Fig. 261).

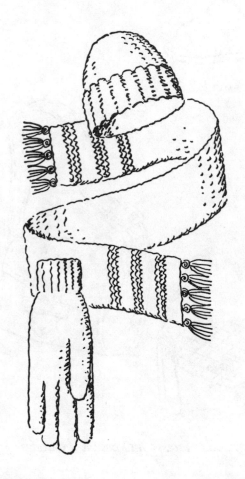

Fig. 261.   Knitted hat, scarf, and gloves

Small accessories to add color and interest are bright silk or synthetic scarves, leather belts, and a few pieces of simple tailored jewelry (Fig. 262).

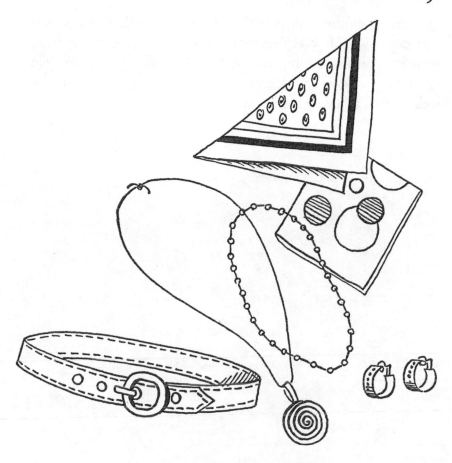

Fig. 262.   Small accessories

This is your basic wardrobe, and most of these items will last a long time. Occasionally you may want to add jazzier items: a bulky cardigan, fancy vests, knickers or gaucho pants.

The warm-weather wardrobe plan is similar, but with the emphasis on lighter colors, cotton fabrics, shorts, and sandals.

Styles change, but the basic wardrobe plan always works,

and classic clothes will never be really outdated. Every season you can add a few replacements and accessories for a fresh new look, while keeping the best of the old. And when you learn to sew your own pants and other clothes, you will be well dressed at a very moderate cost.

BARBARA CORRIGAN loves to sew. In fact, she's been sewing since childhood and now teaches sewing to adults and children, in addition to being a professional dressmaker and designer. Ms. Corrigan, who has lived in Attleboro, Massachusetts, all her life, graduated from the Massachusetts College of Art and worked for many years as a free-lance designer and illustrator for books, advertising, and greeting cards. She is the author of three other books on sewing published by Doubleday, including *Of Course You Can Sew* and *I Love to Sew*.